PORTFOLIO

THE RANBAXY STORY

The Ranbaxy Story is Bhupesh Bhandari's first book, though readers of business news will be familiar with his byline in *Businessworld* and *Business Standard*. Yet to face a dull moment in life, he reads about The Great Game on Sundays and often dreams of going back one day to the mountains from where he hails.

The Ranbaxy Story

The Rise of an Indian Multinational

BHUPESH BHANDARI

PENGUIN
PORTFOLIO

PORTFOLIO
Published by the Penguin Group
Penguin Books India Pvt Ltd, 11 Community Centre, Panchsheel Park,
New Delhi 110 017, India
Penguin Group (USA) Inc., 375 Hudson Street, New York,
New York 10014, USA
Penguin Group (Canada), 90 Eglinton Avenue East, Suite 700, Toronto,
Ontario, M4P 2Y3, Canada (a division of Pearson Penguin Canada Inc.)
Penguin Books Ltd, 80 Strand, London WC2R 0RL, England
Penguin Ireland, 25 St Stephen's Green, Dublin 2, Ireland
(a division of Penguin Books Ltd)
Penguin Group (Australia), 250 Camberwell Road, Camberwell,
Victoria 3124, Australia (a division of Pearson Australia Group Pty Ltd)
Penguin Group (NZ), cnr Airborne and Rosedale Roads, Albany,
Auckland 1310, New Zealand (a division of Pearson New Zealand Ltd)
Penguin Group (South Africa) (Pty) Ltd, 24 Sturdee Avenue, Rosebank,
Johannesburg 2196, South Africa

Penguin Books Ltd, Registered Offices: 80 Strand, London WC2R 0RL, England

First published in Viking by Penguin Books India 2005
Published in paperback in Portfolio 2006

10 9 8 7 6 5 4 3 2 1

ISBN-13: 978-0-14400-097-5 ISBN-10: 0-14400-097-0

Typeset in *Sabon Roman* by SÜRYA, New Delhi
Printed at Chaman Offset Printers, New Delhi

To my father, Col. N.K. Bhandari

Contents

1

Introduction

On Thursday, 21 August 2003, shares of Pfizer Inc., the world's largest pharmaceutical company, fell by 4 per cent, shaving off $7 billion from its market capitalization. This was preceded, the same day, by the investment banking firm Smith Barney cutting its rating on Pfizer after concluding that its largest selling drug, Lipitor, may soon be under threat from a cheaper clone from India's Ranbaxy Laboratories Ltd. 'We disagree with the consensus view that the Lipitor patent challenge is "frivolous",' Smith Barney analyst George Grofik said in a report. 'After reviewing the relevant court documents and consulting our patent attorney, we believe there are significant risks to the Lipitor patent estate.'

Grofik cut his rating on Pfizer from 'outperform' to 'in-line'. Smith Barney also removed the New York-based company from its 'recommended' list. Grofik said the arrival of a generic alternative to Lipitor could coincide with a similar risk to several of the company's other blockbuster drugs, including the antidepressant Zoloft, the antibiotic Zithromax, hypertension drug Norvasc and allergy drug Zyrtec, the patent protection on all of which are to end between 2005 and 2007. The term generic refers to those drugs the patent on which has lapsed and they are no longer protected by a registered trademark. Any drug company is free to manufacture and market them.

Pfizer faced the prospect of a serious dent in its business, thanks to a small Indian company operating out of the cramped and congested commercial district of Nehru Place in New Delhi. While Pfizer reported sales of $32.4 billion in 2002, at the time it made the Lipitor challenge, Ranbaxy had yet to touch a turnover of $1 billion and was hoping to close 2003 at around $950 million. Pfizer's research and development budget of $7.1 billion in 2002 was more than 190 times Ranbaxy's budget of $37 million.

Pfizer—which traces its origin to a modest red brick building in the Williamsburg section of Brooklyn, New York, in 1849—immediately dismissed the Smith Barney report. But it had reasons to be anxious. Lipitor (flucanozole atorvastatin), the world's most prescribed drug for lowering cholesterol, was an innovation of Warner-Lambert Co., the result of painstaking research for thirteen years. Even while the drug was in the development stage, Pfizer knew it had the potential to become a blockbuster. The company first got into a co-marketing alliance with Warner-Lambert to launch Lipitor in the American market in 1997. But the initial reports on the drug were too good to share the profits. With Lipitor in mind, Pfizer eventually took over Warner-Lambert in 2000. Pfizer's gamble paid off: Lipitor recorded sales of $6 billion in 2000, before jumping to $8.6 billion in 2002. It was the crown jewel in Pfizer's portfolio.

In early 2003, Ranbaxy approached the United States Food and Drug Administration (USFDA) for approval to launch its version of flucanozole atorvastatin. Under existing guidelines, the USFDA cannot take more than thirty months to approve a drug after the application is filed, if the bio-equivalence and bio-availability reports are satisfactory. If USFDA finds that the drug has the same results as that of Pfizer's, it can allow Ranbaxy to launch the drug by late-2005. Pfizer's patents on the drug run till 2011. Ranbaxy has challenged two of these, which were extended from 2006 to 2008 and 2010. Pfizer in turn has filed two suits against Ranbaxy in the district court in Delaware for patent infringement.

It is now for the American courts to decide when Pfizer's patent on the drug expires and generic versions of Lipitor can be launched. Whatever the dates fixed by the courts, Ranbaxy will be the first to launch generic flucanozole atorvastatin. Others can follow only after it has had a free run for 180 days. Thus, Ranbaxy will have no competition for six months. Lipitor has achieved a turnover of $10 billion. Once the patent expires in 2008, prices could crash by up to 60 per cent, shrinking the drug's turnover to $4 billion. Ranbaxy can hope to get at least a quarter of this market, or about $1 billion in turnover, during that year.

By 2007, drugs with sales worth $55–60 billion are expected to go off-patent. The business opportunities running into billions of dollars that this opens up for generic companies has led to a race amongst the world's leading producers of generic medicine to become the first-to-file for any drug. Ranbaxy is a leading player in this global game. In 2002 and 2003, no other company (including Israel's Teva Pharmaceutical Industries, the world's largest generics company) had filed more patent applications with USFDA to launch generic drugs than Ranbaxy. Though Lipitor is the biggest drug targeted by Ranbaxy, by the end of 2003 the company was claiming that it could have first-to-file approvals for nine such drugs.

Every quarter, the USFDA releases the list of applications for generic drugs. By monitoring it carefully, pharmaceutical companies the world over find out who has filed first to get the first mover's advantage. A detailed study of these lists gave Ranbaxy reasons to believe that it would be the first to launch nine generic drugs in the United States over the next few years. Apart from Lipitor, the list includes at least one more drug with sales of over a billion dollars—simvastatin 80 mg—which recorded sales of $1.4 billion in 2002.

The Lipitor opportunity was identified early by Ranbaxy. In 2000, Devinder Singh Brar, the then managing director and chief executive officer (CEO), had set up a multidisciplinary committee within the company to look beyond routine filings with USFDA to launch generic drugs. Over the years, Big Pharma, the collective label for the world's top pharmaceutical companies, had been extending patents on bestseller drugs in order to protect their profits, a practice known as the evergreening of patents. Brar knew that often an extension for patents was taken on grounds that could be challenged in a court of law. The committee that he formed had the brief to identify the drugs where patents could be challenged and Ranbaxy could be the first-to-file for a generic version. The committee met every quarter after the members had done an in-depth study of the patents of several drugs. One such drug was Lipitor.

Ranbaxy felt that two of Pfizer's patents on Lipitor could be challenged. Confident of its position, the company's scientists started work on developing a generic version of the drug. The day after the scientists reported that they had developed flucanozole atorvastatin, a Ranbaxy functionary flew out of Delhi to the United States and filed for USFDA approval the very next day. Speed, in the business of generics, is the deciding factor. And Ranbaxy had proved it could beat all others in the game.

*

On 22 October 2003, the board of directors of Ranbaxy had met in Delhi to place on record the company's financial results for the quarter ending September 30. The results were sent to leading publications in India and abroad in the afternoon. The numbers were good and in line with expectations. Even as journalists and research analysts were poring over the results, Paresh Chaudhry, Ranbaxy's energetic head of communications, called up Ranbaxy trackers to tell them to hold their stories—bigger news was on its way. Ranbaxy and GlaxoSmithKline Plc (GSK) had entered into a drug discovery and clinical development collaboration covering a wide range of therapeutic areas. Business newspapers had found their leading story of the day. The next morning's papers carried the announcement prominently.

This was GSK's first collaboration in the developing world, though it has two such tie-ups in Japan, one each with A. Shiniogi and Tanabe Seiyaku. For Ranbaxy, it was nothing short of a coup.

Headquartered in the United Kingdom and with operations based in the United States, GSK has an estimated 7 per cent share of the world's pharmaceutical market and is in a leadership position in four major therapeutic areas—anti-infectives, central nervous system drugs, respiratory drugs and gastro-intestinal/metabolic drugs. In addition, it is a leader in the important area of vaccines and has a growing portfolio of oncology products. Based on the 2002 annual results, GSK had sales of $31.8 billion and profit before tax of $9.7 billion. GSK has over 1,00,000 employees worldwide and its research and development unit is based at twenty-four sites in seven countries and has a budget of $4 billion.

GSK came into being in 2000 after a century of mergers of drug companies beginning in 1891, when Smith, Kline & Company acquired French, Richards & Company to become Smith Kline & French Company. Over the years, the various constituents of GSK had come out with a number of pathbreaking treatments, collecting a string of Nobel awards in the process. But since the early 1990s, like all other Big Pharma companies, it was faced with the prospect of rising research and development costs, coupled with a fall in productivity. As compared to $500 million a decade ago, the cost of developing a new chemical entity had risen to between $800 million and $1 billion by the turn of the century. Like all other big pharmaceutical companies, GSK was looking at ways and means to contain these costs, while driving up productivity. One way of doing it was by forging alliances with low-cost companies with proven scientific skills. As a result, GSK started scouting for opportunities in India, kicking off discussions with a handful of companies like Hyderabad-based Dr Reddy's Laboratories, Ahmedabad-based Torrent Laboratories and Ranbaxy.

Around the same time, Ranbaxy was seriously considering becoming a research-based company with its own pipeline of products. One way was to diligently pursue its own research and development programme. But that would be a time-consuming process. Besides, the costs involved could be astronomical, much more than Ranbaxy could afford. The learning process could be shortened if Ranbaxy could join hands with some multinational research company.

Soon after he took over as Ranbaxy's head of research in 2002, Rashmi Barbhaiya, an American citizen, started sounding out companies abroad for such an alliance. One of the first companies he contacted was GSK. In late 2002, he set up a meeting with Prof. Tamaqua Yamada, GSK's head of research, at Philadelphia in the United States. The two scientists had heard of each other and hit it off instantly. Once the meeting got over and they shook hands, Barbhaiya could see the deal he had in mind taking shape.

It was now left for Ranbaxy vice-president (global licencing) Sanjiv Kaul and his team to take the negotiations to their logical conclusion. Kaul made innumerable trips to the United States, while three different teams from GSK came to India to carry out a due diligence on Ranbaxy, especially its research and development capabilities.

The commercialization of a new chemical entity involves two processes—discovery and development through clinical trials. Initially, GSK wanted to involve Ranbaxy only in the late-discovery part, which meant that leads thrown up by its scientists could be tested more rigorously at Ranbaxy's laboratories. But seeing Ranbaxy's skills, the partnership finally included early development work as well. The deal was sealed in ten months flat.

Several collaborative scenarios were envisioned, with GSK and Ranbaxy leveraging their respective resources and expertise. Under the terms of the agreement, Ranbaxy would be responsible for activities from optimization of a lead compound to generation of a development candidate; leads could be provided by either of the two partners. For a proportion of the candidates selected within the collaboration, Ranbaxy was expected to conduct early clinical work. GSK and Ranbaxy would form an Executive Steering Committee to oversee the research. Once a compound is selected as a development candidate, in most instances GSK would complete development and have the exclusive commercialization responsibilities worldwide, while Ranbaxy will take the lead in India. Ranbaxy, with the consent of GSK, may co-promote in the United States and the European Union. The financial terms of the agreement were not disclosed, though Ranbaxy would be entitled to a royalty on sales of co-developed products including milestone payments.

GSK and Ranbaxy came together even though they were locked in legal battles in the United States, with GSK alleging that Ranbaxy and a few other generic companies used stolen bacteria to come out with generic versions of its bestseller drug Augmentin—a charge Ranbaxy denied. However, at no point, did the matter affect the negotiations for the research and development collaboration. 'It was a humbling experience,' Kaul said after the deal was inked. More to the point, Ranbaxy now was a business partner of an entity no less than GSK. Soon after the deal had been signed, Kaul got an offer to take over as the chief executive of a Big Pharma company in India. He turned down the offer and decided to stay back. No other place could offer him the same excitement as Ranbaxy. He was not prepared to trade it for anything else.

*

Fifth January 2004 was a cold and bleak day in New Delhi. The sun had not come out for a few days and the chill in the air seeped into the bones. But the exhilaration in Brian Tempest's voice was palpable. Talking on the phone from Paris, Ranbaxy's fortnight-old joint managing director and CEO-designate (he had been given this designation on 22 December 2003) was finding it difficult to control his excitement: 'As we talk, we are booking sales on Ranbaxy's name. We are the fifth largest generics player in France.'

Tempest, a British national who had taken to India and Ranbaxy like fish to water, had just inked the deal on the acquisition of RPG Aventis, the generics arm of French firm Aventis. Valued at $65–70 million, this was the largest overseas acquisition by any Indian pharmaceutical company and the normally soft-spoken and measured Tempest's excitement was only natural.

Ranbaxy had been working on the deal for several months, and had closed in on it by the end of 2003. RPG Aventis, a 100 per cent subsidiary of Aventis, was the fifth largest generic company in France with an annual turnover of 55–60 million euro. The acquisition catapulted Ranbaxy to among the top generic companies in that country.

Europe accounts for 25 per cent of the world pharmaceutical market, with the United Kingdom, Germany and France being the three most lucrative markets on the continent. Ranbaxy was already well entrenched in the United Kingdom and had also acquired a manufacturing unit with a certification laboratory in Ireland. In Germany, it had a toehold in the generics market, with its acquisition of Basics GmbH, the generics arm of Bayer AG. It then started eyeing the French generics market.

Like elsewhere in the developed world, the French government had taken steps to encourage generic medicine in order to bring down the cost of healthcare. In a trailblazing move, it had empowered chemists to sell a generic medicine even if the doctor had prescribed a patented drug. Estimated at $700–800 million in 2003, the generics market in France was projected to grow at 45 per cent per annum to reach a size of $6 billion by 2008. Ranbaxy could hardly ignore this market. At the same time, it had come to the conclusion that an organic growth model would not work in the country, since it could take up to twenty-eight months for a new company to get its products approved for a launch. The only way out was to acquire a generics company as fast as possible.

Ranbaxy began looking for a mid-sized company in France. It initiated negotiations with two—Irex and RPG Aventis—but found that the latter had a better portfolio of products and a good pipeline of products for a future launch. Talks with Irex were abandoned and Ranbaxy decided to focus on RPG Aventis. Though Aventis was not too keen to divest its stake in the company, it had announced that it wanted to bow out of the generics business in order to focus on its proprietary products.

In late-2003, Aventis had more than forty compounds in clinical development, including over twenty-five in early-stage clinical development and more than fifteen in late-stage development. By taking early data-driven decisions, it planned to optimize and prioritize its compound portfolio so as to increase the success potential and, hence, the value of its pipeline. In addition, it was actively pursuing attractive in-licensing opportunities and alliances to strengthen its leading positions in disease areas such as oncology (treatment of tumors), diabetes, thrombosis (coagulation or clotting of blood) and in vaccines. Headquartered at Strasbourg in France, Aventis has under its belt brands like Allegra and Telfast for the treatment of allergies, Lovenox and Clexane for thrombosis, Taxotere in the field of oncology, Delix and Tritace for hypertension, Actonel for osteoporosis and Lantus for diabetes.

Aventis was formed in 1999 when Hoechst AG of Germany and Rhône-Poulenc S.A. of France—two companies with rich histories spanning over 100 years and experience in markets throughout the world—came together. Aventis is a world leader in the discovery, development and marketing of innovative pharmaceutical products. Its core business comprises prescription drugs and human vaccines as well as the animal health business in the form of Merial, a fifty-fifty joint venture with Merck & Co. In 2002, its core business sales were to the tune of 17.59 billion euro. Its research and development spending during the year totalled 3.14 billion euro, or 17.9 per cent of its core business sales. Aventis's research and development efforts are focussed on delivering innovations for therapeutic areas such as respiratory ailments/allergy, cardiovascular disease, oncology, diabetes and human vaccines.

Once it became known that Aventis wanted to opt out of the generics business and RPG Aventis could be on the block, several pharmaceutical companies from across the world, including others from India, had jumped into the fray. In the end, Ranbaxy emerged the winner. Unlike in the United States, the generic space in France was not too cluttered. The top ten companies account for almost 85 per cent of the market. As a result, the RPG Aventis acquisition helped Ranbaxy establish a critical mass in the country in double quick time.

The acquisition did wonders to Ranbaxy's image. It was soon flooded with similar offers. One of these was for Heumann of Germany. However, Ranbaxy had its sights trained on something else. The same day that he completed the RPG Aventis acquisition, Tempest announced that his next target was a brand in the United States. 'It could either be a brand or a company owning a brand,' he said. The brand would be niche and small and in the therapeutic areas of antibiotics or urology, Ranbaxy's traditional strengths.

Aided by the takeover of RPG Aventis, Ranbaxy's twelve-month sales crossed $1 billion in February 2004.

*

The ceremony at the World Economic Forum Headquarters at Cologny, Geneva, in April 2003 was elaborate. Dr René Imhof, the head of pharmaceutical research at Switzerland-based Hoffman-La Roche, symbolically handed over a baton to Barbhaiya. As soon as the baton passed hands, Ranbaxy had replaced Roche as the pharmaceutical partner in the synthetic peroxide project of the Medicines for Malaria Venture (MMV).

MMV had been officially launched on 3 November 1999 as a non-profit foundation dedicated to reducing the burden of malaria in 'disease endemic' countries by discovering new affordable anti-malarial drugs through effective public-private partnerships. The major obstacle to the discovery of new anti-malarials is the lack of global investment in drug research and development. The enormous costs and time needed for research and development, and the little or sometimes no prospect of return on investment once a drug is fully registered and on the market, discourage the large pharmaceutical companies from entering the field. MMV's origins lie in the failure of the market system to provide the required incentives for large-scale research and development in new medicines to treat malaria.

MMV receives funding and support from the Bill and Melinda Gates Foundation, Exxon-Mobil Corporation, Global Forum for Health Research, International Federation of Pharmaceutical Manufacturers Associations, Netherlands Ministry for Development Cooperation, Rockefeller Foundation, Swiss Agency for Development and Cooperation, United Kingdom's Department for International Development (DFID), World Bank, the Roll Back Malaria programme of the World Health Organization (WHO), United Nations Development Programme (UNDP)/World Bank/WHO Special Programme for Research and Training in Tropical Diseases (TDR) and the Wellcome Trust.

By mid-2003, MMV was managing a portfolio of over fourteen projects in different stages of drug research and development. The most ambitious of these was the synthetic peroxide project, named the 'Project of the Year' in 2001 by MMV's Expert Scientific Advisory Committee. Roche had been a partner in the project for three years. Now Roche was out and Ranbaxy was in. Barbhaiya took over in the presence of the members of the board and the leading stakeholders of MMV.

Commenting on the occasion, Dr Christopher Hentschel, CEO, MMV, said, 'Ranbaxy is the ideal partner to drive this project forward. The company has demonstrated skills and expertise to discover new molecules, and take them through the process of development and also conduct clinical trials to international standards. Their presence in several African countries makes them the right partner for MMV in achieving its mission to discover, develop and deliver medicines to the "disease endemic" countries, at affordable cost.' The discovery team for this innovative molecule comprised leading scientists from the University of Nebraska Medical Centre, Monash University and the Swiss Tropical Institute with the active participation and support of Roche, working on the MMV's partnership model. This project has now advanced to the point where a new anti-malarial compound can be proposed for further technical and clinical development.

The drug candidates identified so far in the project were

showing outstanding anti-malarial activity and superior pharmacokinetic (movement of drug within the body) and ADME (absorption, distribution, metabolism and excretion) properties. Ranbaxy would now carry out the development and file an IND (Investigational New Drug) application, once it established efficacy and safety in the pre-clinical phase. The new molecule should ensure a short treatment period of three days for malaria, and the cost of the product is expected to be much less than the presently used artemisinin derivatives, using naturally grown *Artemisia annua* plants.

Headquartered in Basel, Switzerland, Roche is one of the world's leading innovation-driven healthcare groups. Its core businesses are pharmaceuticals and diagnostics and the company is number one in the global diagnostics market, the leading supplier of pharmaceuticals for cancer and a leader in virology and transplantation. As a supplier of products and services for the prevention, diagnosis and treatment of disease, the group contributes on a broad range of fronts to improving people's health and quality of life. Roche employs roughly 62,000 people in 150 countries. The group has alliances and research and development agreements with numerous partners, including majority ownership interests in San Francisco-based Genentech Inc. and Tokyo-based Chugai Pharmaceuticals. With such impeccable credentials, how was Ranbaxy able to replace Roche in the MMV venture?

Actually, there was little left in the venture to interest Roche. Malaria has been more or less eradicated in the developed world and is now confined to tropical climates in Africa. The overall market for anti-malaria drugs is not more than $600 million. Roche had decided to devote its energies to other therapeutic segments.

P.V. Venugopal, who had earlier worked for Dr Reddy's Laboratories, had joined MMV as director of international operations in March 2001. (Later, R.A. Mashelkar, the director-general of the Council of Scientific and Industrial

Research, also joined the MMV board.) Once it became clear that Roche wanted to exit from the venture, Venugopal saw this as an opportunity to get an Indian company in. Even when he was working for Dr Reddy's Laboratories, he had developed a healthy respect for Ranbaxy and its team of scientists and had, in fact, unsuccessfully tried to bring the two companies together. He first approached Ranbaxy with the proposal for the MMV project. Initially, Ranbaxy was cold to the proposal.

When Barbhaiya took over as the head of research and development in Ranbaxy in 2002, a farewell dinner was organized for his predecessor, Jag Mohan Khanna, who had retired. At the dinner, Venugopal drew Barbhaiya aside and brought up the MMV proposal one more time. This time the idea clicked and Barbhaiya agreed to take over the project from Roche. Ranbaxy's research and development strengths in process chemistry, formulation development and other pre-clinical expertise, strong regulatory submission capabilities and cost-effectiveness were the key considerations for MMV to partner with the company.

Despite being aware that the market for anti-malaria drugs would not run into billions of dollars, Ranbaxy took on the project because it would gain the experience of carrying out the development of a drug through clinical trials. This was a big leap forward for the company. It had come out with a new chemical entity for the treatment of benign prostatic hyperplasia (BPH), the enlargement of prostate gland in men, but could not take it through the development process on account of the high costs involved and had to license it to Schwarz of Germany. But clinical trials for MMV's anti-malaria drug would not entail huge costs, as these would have to be carried out in tropical Africa where the cost of involving doctors and patients would be much lower than in the West.

An elated Barbhaiya said after taking over, 'Ranbaxy's alliance with MMV is a manifestation of its emerging profile as an integrated research player. I am confident that this venture will help the world gain from Ranbaxy's research and development skills, as well as allow us to fully leverage our entire span of research and commercial infrastructure.' Ranbaxy had another feather in its cap.

*

On 21 November 2003, the Ranbaxy research and development centre at Gurgaon, on the outskirts of Delhi, had an important visitor. Bill Clinton, the former American President, was on a short visit to India. Apart from meeting the prime minister, Atal Behari Vajpayee, with whom he had struck a warm friendship during his tenure at the White House, Clinton took time out to visit Ranbaxy's research facility. Spread across two buildings, this wing of Ranbaxy has about a thousand people on its rolls. Throughout 2003, it was hiring three to four scientists a week on an average. There was a purpose behind Clinton's visit. He wanted to assure himself that all the talk about the company's scientific skills was not exaggerated.

A few weeks before that, the William J. Clinton Presidential Foundation had announced that it had tied up with four companies worldwide to supply anti-AIDS medicine in poor African countries. Three of the four were Indian companies—Mumbai-based Cipla, Hyderabad-based Matrix Laboratories and Ranbaxy. India's campaign for cheap anti-AIDS medicine had finally borne fruit.

It all began in 2000 when Yusuf Hamied, chairman of Cipla India Limited, offered to sell anti-retroviral drugs for treatment of HIV/AIDS at a fraction of existing prices. He told a European Commission medical meeting in Brussels that he could sell a three-drug anti-retroviral combination for around $800 per patient per year, while Big Pharma was selling its combination for nothing less than $12,000 per patient per year. In 2001, he turned the knife by further dropping his prices to $300 per patient per year. There was more to come. He finally offered to sell the three-drug anti-AIDS cocktail for $140 per patient per year 'subject to some conditions'. The whole world applauded his bold initiative. Hamied had brought to the notice of one and all that India had the wherewithal to help poor countries in Africa to fight the growing AIDS menace.

Hamied was born with fire in his belly. His father, Khwaja Abdul Hamied, had become a firebrand nationalist when he was just fifteen. In the infamous Kanpur Mosque incident of 1913, the police had shot at hundreds of people in a mosque close to where he lived. The senior Hamied was present at the gathering and just about managed to escape unhurt. This first-hand experience of imperial high-handedness filled him with deep hatred for foreign rule. After earning his doctorate from Berlin University in 1927 (his thesis topic was: The Technology of Barium Compounds), Hamied returned to India with a dream to start an Indian pharmaceutical company. In 1935, he set up The Chemical, Industrial & Pharmaceutical Laboratories, which came to be popularly known as Cipla. He gave the company all his patent and proprietary formulae for several drugs and medicines, without charging any royalty. Sixty-five years later, Cipla stunned the world with Yusuf Hamied's audacious offer on the anti-HIV drugs.

Ranbaxy was quick to latch on to Cipla's vision that Indian companies would engage in the development of low-cost anti-retrovirals. The initiative would also give a big boost to the company's corporate social responsibility programme. The world over, pharmaceutical companies invest heavily in image building. Drugs can often go wrong, causing pain and misery, and a small incident can cause permanent damage to a company's reputation. That is why pharmaceutical companies spend large sums of money to present their humane face to the world. Ranbaxy was not going to let the opportunity pass it by.

The problem was, even at the dirt-cheap rates offered by Indian companies, the developing countries could not afford to place large orders for anti-AIDS drugs. With the orders not coming in, companies were not investing in building up capacities. Till the Clinton Foundation stepped in. From the time he demitted office in January 2001, Clinton, in conjunction with the Clinton Presidential Foundation, had continued work on many issues that defined his administration, including the economic empowerment of the poor; racial, ethnic and religious reconciliation; and the education and health of young people.

Clinton had made the battle against AIDS a focal point of his activities and had set up the Clinton Foundation HIV/AIDS Initiative. This initiative aims to assist nations in implementing large-scale integrated care, treatment and prevention programmes to turn the tide of the AIDS epidemic. It partners with countries in Africa and the Caribbean to develop operational business plans to scale-up AIDS treatment. Nearly 40 million people are infected with HIV/AIDS in the developing world.

Since the resource-poor countries lack the funds to carry out effective care and treatment programmes and do not have the required infrastructure, nearly all AIDS treatment programmes in these countries tend to be small-scale pilot projects, often carried out by non-governmental organizations (NGOs) that are outside the mainstream health systems. According to the Clinton Foundation, while these pilot programmes are important, they cannot provide the solution for whole countries. Their efforts must be coordinated and the mainstream health infrastructure substantially upgraded to aggressively address the issue of HIV/AIDS. To this effect, the foundation is arranging donations for these poor countries, while assisting their governments draw up an effective management plan for the treatment of the pandemic.

Clinton first approached Big Pharma: would it supply anti-AIDS drugs for Africa at low prices? The response was lukewarm. These companies were willing to drop their prices only marginally. With little progress in sight, Clinton decided to source the medicine from Indian companies. Big Pharma was both horrified and scared. What if the same medicine somehow found its way to non-African markets? Steamrolling their opposition, key Clinton aides started calling up Indian pharmaceutical companies.

This was just the platform Ranbaxy needed. Its anti-AIDS business was plagued by the uncertainty over payments and skirmishes with Big Pharma over patents. But with the Clinton Foundation in the picture, the payments would be secured. During the Doha Ministerial Round of the World Trade Organization (WTO) in November 2001, it was agreed that poor countries would be allowed to import patented medicine by issuing licences to low-cost producers in case of an epidemic. But there were apprehensions that these countries could be armtwisted to issue these licences to either Big Pharma or its affiliates in the developing world. With the Clinton Foundation getting involved, these fears subsided.

Though the margins on anti-AIDS medicine had become wafer-thin, the volumes could now be large. The Clinton Foundation plans to scale up the number of patients brought under treatment from 75,000 to 1.5 million by 2008, by when the supplies required are expected to touch $175 million. Ranbaxy can hope to corner a fourth of this business, or roughly $40–45 million. Its anti-AIDS business had finally taken off to a flying start.

*

On 20 December 2003, soon after he came out of New Delhi's Indira Gandhi International Airport, Ranbaxy chairman Tejinder Khanna started getting calls on his cell phone from other Ranbaxy directors. Brar's term as the managing director and CEO of the company was coming to an end on 4 July 2004 and he had hinted that he was not interested in renewing his term. The matter was likely to come up at the board meeting on 22 December.

Khanna, a former bureaucrat, had only two days to take stock of the situation, having been overseas for over a month. Khanna resisted all temptation to call Brar and check with the man himself. Instead, he decided to let the events unfold on their own.

On the appointed day, Brar announced that he would like to step down. He was perfectly in control and his voice did not betray any emotion. No sooner had his short speech ended, than Khanna asked him to name his successor. Without a moment's hesitation, Brar named Tempest. What about the vacancy created by Tempest, Khanna asked. Brar said it would be Malvinder 'Malav' Mohan Singh, the elder of the two sons of the late Parvinder Singh. Malav and his brother, Shivinder Mohan Singh, are Ranbaxy's principal shareholders with a 32 per cent stake in the company. Thus, Malav was to become president (pharmaceuticals) from 1 January 2004. Along with the job came a berth on the board. The board meeting, which saw the third transition of power at Ranbaxy, was soon over.

Malav, who was sitting in his office, got a call from Brar and went to meet him. The two men hugged and Brar congratulated Malav. Not able to control his emotions, Malav broke down.

Meanwhile, the news spread like wildfire. Brar, after all, was the best-known figure in the Indian pharmaceutical industry. He was also the public face of Indian multinationals and part of a strong bunch of intrepid men not willing to let their ambitions be stifled by their national boundaries. Just a few months earlier, Brar and other senior Ranbaxy functionaries had flown to Mumbai to collect the Company of the Year award from the *Economic Times*. The Confederation of Indian Industry (CII), the country's most influential industry association and lobby group, had set up a committee to help Indian companies go global, which was a kind of a preparatory school for Indian multinationals. Brar was the undisputed choice as the leader of this committee.

Within Ranbaxy, there was an unprecedented outpouring of emotion. Brar was flooded with e-mails from staffers all across the world. In the weeks that followed, several key Ranbaxy functionaries left the company, uncertain about the company's future without Brar at the helm. Among those who quit were Barbhaiya and Kaul.

Tempest, recently back from England, where he had taken his wife, Jasmine, for treatment, had hit the high-water mark of his career. It was the culmination of a long journey for Tempest. The son of a barber from Morecambe near the Lake District in England, Tempest had had no connection with India—none of his ancestors or relatives had served in the country during the Raj. After getting a Ph.D in Chemistry from Lancaster University, Tempest started his career in the pharmaceuticals industry, signing up with Beecham. He worked there for fourteen years before moving on to Glaxo and from there to GD Searle.

In 1995, when Ranbaxy decided to go for rapid expansion internationally, it needed people with global experience in key overseas positions. Tempest was identified by the executive search firm of Micky Daulat Singh, a childhood friend of Dr Singh and a member of the Ranbaxy board of directors. At the time he was the worldwide commerical operations director of Fisons Plc, running the company's operations in forty countries.

After a meeting with Dr Singh at a lakeside hotel in Geneva, Tempest was on board as regional director for Europe, CIS and Africa. In January 2000 he was promoted as worldwide president (pharmaceuticals) and transferred from London to New Delhi. The new job came with a slot on the company's board. And in December 2003, he was elevated to the driving seat.

Malav, on his part, found no time for celebrations. A few days later, he took the train to Beas, a small town between Jalandhar and Amritsar in Punjab, to spend a few days with his spiritual guru.

Meanwhile, in a spacious and lonely bungalow in central Delhi, a warrior was finally getting old. Active till a year ago, he had spent a better part of the year in and out of hospitals. At home, the eighty-four-year-old Sikh, whose tall frame had an imposing presence, was confined to his bed, much to his dislike. His shrivelled form was not even a pale shadow of his old regal bearing. He was Bhai Mohan Singh. He had ruled over Ranbaxy with an iron fist for over four decades.

2

The Early Years

Bhai Mohan Singh was born on 30 December 1917 in a small village called Nareli in the Rawalpindi district of Punjab (now in Pakistan). His father, Bhai Gyan Chand, was a Hindu and his mother, Sunder Dai, a Sikh. However, he was brought up as a Sikh following an incident that occurred soon after he was born.

As was the custom, Sunder Dai had gone to her parents' village to deliver the baby. It was winter and an *angeethi* (charcoal stove) of glowing embers was kept under Sunder Dai's bed to keep both the mother and baby warm. At night, the child fell into the angeethi and sustained severe burns, the marks of which Bhai Mohan Singh has borne on his legs and his back all his life, as he has the pain of those burns. With no doctor for miles around, his parents could only seek divine intervention. They took their child to the village gurdwara, the only place of worship available for Hindus. There, Bhai Gyan Chand vowed that if his son survived, he would make him a Sikh.

Bhai Mohan Singh recovered quickly. When he turned

three, his father, true to his word, made him a Sikh. This led to many of his relatives making their children Sikhs, though they were much older to Bhai Mohan Singh. By the time he was five, Bhai Mohan Singh had started reciting verses from the Guru Granth Sahib. When he was thirteen, Bhai Mohan Singh tried to cut his long hair short. This infuriated his father so much that he made him do penance for over a month. He was given very little food to eat and made to walk barefoot to the gurdwara every day under the blazing sun to atone for his sin.

Bhai Gyan Chand was a descendant of Bhai Gurudas Ji, a disciple of the fifth Sikh guru, Arjan Dev. Gurudas Ji's flair for social service had earned him the title Bhai, which the family continued to use. However, only two of Bhai Mohan Singh's sons—Analjit and Manjit—have used the title. Analjit (he was called BAS—short for Bhai Analjit Singh—by the people in his office) also gave up the prefix in the late-1990s. None of Bhai Mohan Singh's grandchildren use the prefix.

*

Bhai Gyan Chand started as a farmer at Khalsabhaiyan village in the Jhelum district of Punjab (now in Pakistan). Later, along with his brother, Bhai Sunder Dass, he set up a civil construction business taking up government contracts between Rawalpindi and Peshawar in the North West Frontier Province. Bhai Sunder Dass soon shifted base to Jhelum in order to handle the business better and Bhai Gyan Chand followed him a few years later. The brothers built houses on adjacent plots. The two houses were connected by a corridor and there was a common kitchen for both the families. Apart from filial love, the brothers were bound also by the fact that their wives were sisters.

As their business prospered, Bhai Gyan Chand moved once again from Jhelum to the upscale Rawalpindi

Cantonment in 1941. Now that he was doing well—he had a fleet of cars and horse-driven carriages—he could afford to be close to the corridors of power in order to bag government contracts.

Meanwhile, after completing his Senior Cambridge from Rawalpindi, Bhai Mohan Singh had enrolled in Government College, Lahore, for his graduation, and moved into a hostel. His friends from those days—Prem Pandhi, who went on to become the chairman of Cadbury India, and O.P. Mehra, who was to later command the Indian Air Force, to name just two—would remember him as an easy-going and helpful person, though not an exceptional student. More important, he did nothing to flaunt the fact that he was a rich man's son (his father gifted him a brand-new Austin when he passed out of Government College).

The very next year, Bhai Mohan Singh married Avtar Kaur, the daughter of an influential Rawalpindi lawyer, Sardar Bahadur Bakshi Dalip Singh. During the last years of the British Raj, Bakshi Dalip Singh's name was recommended for knighthood. But the British left before his name could be taken up and he was never knighted. After Partition, Bakshi Dalip Singh moved to Mumbai (then Bombay) where he rose quickly in social stature and went on to become the mayor of the city.

After passing out of college in 1941, Bhai Mohan Singh was reluctant to join his father's business. However, Bhai Gyan Chand persuaded him to do so. The family construction firm now had a new name—Bhai Gyan Chand Mohan Singh. The Second World War was raging and British colonies like India found themselves sucked into the conflict. This brought an unexpected windfall for firms like Bhai Gyan Chand Mohan Singh in the form of huge civil construction contracts from the Military Engineering Services (MES). The first MES contract came almost immediately after Bhai Mohan Singh had joined the family firm. The army was trying to build barracks for its soldiers at Yol

Camp near Dharamsala in the picturesque Kangra valley of present-day Himachal Pradesh. The earlier contractor had bungled and the authorities decided to give the contract to Bhai Gyan Chand Mohan Singh.

As it was their first MES contract, father and son left no stone unturned to complete the work to the satisfaction of the authorities. They obviously had an eye on more such contracts while the war lasted. Bhai Gyan Chand stationed his son at Nagrota railway station in Kangra valley to oversee the landing of timber and cement by train and their dispatch for Yol Camp by road. This was to be Bhai Mohan Singh's first exposure to the world of business.

The efforts put in by the father-and-son team paid off. This contract was followed by another one from the army headquarters in Delhi for the civil engineering work for an aerodrome at Agra. This work was finished in a year and a half. By now, the family had made it big. Bhai Mohan Singh got a membership into the elite Rawalpindi Club where he would rub shoulders with senior officers from the army as well as the civil administration.

Still bigger things were in store for the father-son duo. In 1943, they were summoned to the army headquarters in Delhi to submit a proposal to build a 550 km road connecting Bongaigaon in Assam to the Indian border with Myanmar (then Burma) in Nagaland. The Japanese army was advancing rapidly through Myanmar and the British needed roads to quickly rush its soldiers to the border.

After carrying out an aerial survey of the country from a Dakota provided by the army, Bhai Gyan Chand agreed to execute the contract. Having got the army to agree to a hefty compensation if either of the two was killed and taking an assurance that they would not be required to work within two miles of enemy fire (their workers were actually asked to retreat several times after heavy shelling from the Japanese), Bhai Gyan Chand put in a request for special trains to transport 5,000 mules and seventy trucks from Rawalpindi to Assam. The government gave the firm five special trains.

Work on the highway was soon under way. For the next four years, from 1943 to 1946, Bhai Gyan Chand and his wife shifted base to Shillong to oversee the work. Bhai Mohan Singh remained in Rawalpindi, visiting his parents off and on with his eldest son, Parvinder, who was born in 1943. He was trying to move the firm's business interests closer to Rawalpindi from lawless Peshawar and he was responsible for liaisoning with the authorities and giving a shape to the family's business. From operating out of his two coat pockets, by 1946, Bhai Mohan Singh had over 200 people, including several engineers, working for him at Rawalpindi.

By all accounts, Bhai Gyan Chand Mohan Singh made a sizeable profit in the Rs 25-crore Assam contract. However, even more than fifty years after completing the project, Bhai Mohan Singh was reluctant to disclose the amount. One winter evening in 2002, he let slip that the family paid income tax amounting to Rs 5–6 crore between 1943 and 1946. However, the figure needs to be treated with caution, as in those days there was an excess profit tax of 91.25 per cent. But, clearly, the family had started being counted as one of the wealthiest Punjabi families of the time.

There were other signs to show that the family had arrived. In 1945, a bungalow located at 28 Prithviraj Road in New Delhi had been purchased from an Englishman for Rs 2,50,000. Spread over 2.5 acres, it was set amidst sprawling lawns, had several rooms with extensive woodwork in Burma teak (the earlier owner was in the public works department of the government), a swimming pool, a tennis court as well as stables for horses. Later, Bhai Mohan Singh built another house within the same location and sold off another house within the compound. Bhai Gyan Chand also bought a house each for his three daughters—Wiranwali, Mohan Kaur and Gobind Kaur—in the Karol Bagh area of

Delhi. Each of the three families was to later sell their house and move to an upmarket location in south Delhi.

In August/September 1946, with the work on the highway completed, Bhai Gyan Chand returned to Rawalpindi. A couple of months later, he announced to his son that he wished to retire from business and that he had transferred the money from all his accounts, save one, to Bhai Mohan Singh's account at Lloyds Bank which was located opposite the family house in Rawalpindi Cantonment.

*

Life was being kind to Bhai Mohan Singh. He was moving up the social ladder in Rawalpindi and had made important friends in the army as well as the civil administration. His father-in-law had enrolled him into the Freemasons society and he had become an important office-bearer of its Rawalpindi branch. In January 1947, his wife gave birth to their second son, Manjit.

In March 1947, communal riots erupted in Rawalpindi as in many other places in India after the British made clear their plans to partition the country. On 5 March 1947, Bhai Gyan Chand had sent his son to Delhi to collect some payments due from the government. On reaching Delhi, Bhai Mohan Singh called up their tenant at Prithviraj Road—a Muslim police officer who had served as the superintendent of police at Rawalpindi and was now in-charge of the government's anti-corruption wing in New Delhi. A few days earlier, the tenant had sent a telegram to Bhai Gyan Chand in Rawalpindi saying that he wished to move to Pakistan in the month of May. They agreed to meet the next day.

When they met the next evening over a cup of tea, the tenant informed Bhai Mohan Singh that there had been serious communal riots in Rawalpindi. Bhai Mohan Singh was worried about the welfare and safety of his family. To calm him, the tenant then booked a trunk call to Bhai Gyan Chand. Since he was a high-profile police officer, the call came through right away. Bhai Gyan Chand asked his son to return immediately. As there were no flights within the next two days for Rawalpindi, Bhai Mohan Singh booked a train ticket for himself through the government quota and reached Rawalpindi. His father, escorted by an army guard, was at the railway station to receive him.

Once they reached home, there was a family conclave at which Bhai Sunder Dass and Bakshi Dalip Singh were also present. It was decided that Bhai Mohan Singh should immediately charter an aircraft to evacuate the family from Rawalpindi to the safe confines of New Delhi. Bhai Mohan Singh rushed to Delhi and was back in Rawalpindi with a DC3 aircraft a few days later. But Bhai Gyan Chand and his wife refused to leave because he was the chairman of the Relief Committee formed to look after the Hindus and Sikhs moving to India. Many such people fleeing from their homes in the neighbouring villages had found refuge in the family house.

So Bhai Mohan Singh left for Delhi with his wife and sons, Parvinder and Manjit. On reaching Delhi, he made straight for the Imperial, Delhi's most upmarket hotel at the time, and checked into a suite there, as the tenant was yet to vacate their Prithviraj Road house. The suite had been reserved for Bhai Mohan Singh by Rajdev Singh, the son of Imperial's owner, Sardar Bahadur Ranjit Singh. Rajdev had studied with Bhai Mohan Singh in Lahore and the two had shared a dormitory. The friendship had continued even after school. Both got married within fifteen days of each other. Whenever Rajdev went to Kashmir with his wife, Nirlep Kaur, they would make it a point to stay with Bhai Mohan Singh at Rawalpindi for a couple of days.

Unknown to Bhai Mohan Singh, another businessman, H.P. Nanda, who founded the Delhi-based Escorts group, was also staying in the hotel with his family after being displaced from his home in Pakistan. But unlike Bhai Mohan Singh, he could not afford to stay there. He had only checked into the hotel so that his old business associates did not come to know that he had lost everything in the Partition and they would continue to do business with him.

Bhai Mohan Singh still had his parents at Rawalpindi to worry about and he would take a flight there every Wednesday morning, stay for seven hours, and return to Delhi in the evening. Bhai Gyan Chand and his wife finally came to Delhi only on 8 August 1947, seven days before Independence. He passed away in 1954 just when Bhai Mohan Singh had got into the driving seat at Ranbaxy. However, Sunder Dai lived on till 1983 and was a witness to the first tentative steps taken by Ranbaxy on its march to global status.

As Bhai Mohan Singh had substantial fortunes in Delhi, his house soon became a centre of entertainment for his circle of friends from Pakistan, many of whom had reached Delhi with empty pockets. More importantly, Bhai Mohan Singh quickly went into business, setting up a finance company, Bhai Traders & Financiers Pvt. Ltd, with his father as its chairman, his mother as a director and himself as its managing director. The venture soon turned profitable with the company lending money to several companies. Among them was Ranbaxy & Co. Ltd, a small pharmaceutical agency.

*

In 1937, in the holy city of Amritsar, two cousins, Ranjit Singh and Gurbax Singh, had got together to form a company called Ranbaxy & Co. to take up the distribution of medicines in the country on behalf of foreign pharmaceutical companies. While Ranjit Singh was in the clothing business, Gurbax Singh had worked with the Japanese pharmaceutical company, A. Shiniogi, which made vitamins and anti-tuberculosis (TB) drugs. As Gurbax Singh was known to Shiniogi, it appointed Ranbaxy its distributor for India. Ranbaxy's representatives would travel from one town to another either by train or in a bus carrying their stock in tin trunks and would put up at dharamshalas.

After the Japanese army made rapid advances in south Asia during the Second World War, trade relations between Japan and Great Britain and its colonies were suspended. As a result, Ranbaxy's business came to a standstill for ten years from 1940 to 1950 when India reopened its trade ties with Japan. Once again, Ranbaxy was appointed Shiniogi's sole distributor in India. In addition, it had become a sub-agent for north India of the Kolkata-based Dey's Medical Stores, which belonged to Dr B.C. Roy, who later became chief minister of West Bengal. Dey's Medical Stores was the exclusive dealer in India for the American firm Pfizer. In 1952, Ranbaxy gave up both the agencies in favour of Lepetit SpA of Milan, Italy.

By this time, Ranjit Singh was out of the company and Gurbax Singh had emerged as the sole promoter of Ranbaxy. In addition to the Shiniogi agency, Ranbaxy used to run a small chemist shop in the commercial district of Connaught Place in New Delhi, operating out of 3,000 sq. ft of space just below the Marina Hotel. The company, however, was strapped for cash. In 1951, Gurbax Singh approached Bhai Mohan Singh for a loan of Rs 1,00,000. Subsequently, Bhai Mohan Singh gave two more loans of Rs 1,00,000 each. When Ranbaxy was unable to return the money, Gurbax Singh offered to hand the company over to Bhai Mohan Singh, an offer the latter readily accepted. Bhai Mohan Singh paid Rs 2,50,000 to Gurbax Singh for 200 Ranbaxy shares and became the promoter of Ranbaxy & Co. on 1 August 1952. Soon he had occupied the company's Connaught Place office to which he added a mezzanine floor.

Though he was the managing director of the company,

Bhai Mohan Singh retained Gurbax Singh on the board as the president of the company. This was the first time he was trying his hand at the pharmaceutical business and he needed somebody to guide him. In addition, Sobi-el-Ejal, a Mumbai-based Syrian who was also the honorary consul for Syria, was chairman of the company's board of directors. For the next two years, till 1954, Bhai Mohan Singh managed the affairs of the company. Then he had his first fight with Gurbax Singh.

*

Bhai Gyan Chand passed away in November 1954. Around 11 a.m. on the day of Bhai Gyan Chand's death, Gurbax Singh came to Bhai Mohan Singh's residence to offer his condolences. After telling the grieving Bhai Mohan Singh that he too treated Bhai Gyan Chand like a father (he would call him Papaji), Gurbax Singh said that a board meeting of Ranbaxy had been scheduled for the next day but it had been cancelled due to Bhai Gyan Chand's death.

Almost half a century after their relationship began to sour, Bhai Mohan Singh would love to recount his showdown with Gurbax Singh to the last detail. Though he was bent with age, his aching knees wrapped in a shawl to keep them warm, Bhai Mohan Singh was sharp and alert as ever mentally. He would recall the names of his associates at the time and occasionally fish out some old documents, though he would never part with the papers. What follows is his account of how he gained control of the company.

Bhai Mohan Singh was too involved in arrangements for his father's last rites to take note of Gurbax Singh's seemingly innocuous statement. His sister and her husband, Jaswant Singh (who was to later work for Ranbaxy) were away in Chennai and they needed to be brought back to Delhi for the cremation.

Bhai Gyan Chand was cremated the next day. As soon

as Bhai Mohan Singh returned from the cremation ground at 11.30 a.m., Gurbax Singh called on him. 'Bhai Ji, I have postponed the meeting scheduled for today because of Papaji's death. But there is an important development about which I need to talk to you,' he said, forcing himself on Bhai Mohan Singh. Tired from not having slept the previous night and with an army of relatives to look after, Bhai Mohan Singh tried to wriggle out of the meeting. 'Sleep for three–four hours. We will meet in the afternoon,' Gurbax Singh was persistent. Finally, the two agreed to meet the next morning.

At the meeting the next day, Gurbax Singh suggested that Bhai Mohan Singh take over the Ranbaxy shares left with him and run the company himself. He even offered to resign from the company's board immediately. Bhai Mohan Singh realized that his business partner was a shrewd man. According to Bhai Mohan Singh, Gurbax Singh's line of thinking went something like this: he was aware that Bhai Mohan Singh had no idea of running a pharmaceuticals business. Indeed, that is why he had been retained as the president of the company. He thought that by offering to bow out of the company, he could scare Bhai Mohan Singh into selling out to him at the price of his choice. The time chosen by him to unleash his plan could not have been better: he knew that Bhai Mohan Singh would be somewhat disoriented on the day after his father's death and could, hence, be pushed to take such a decision.

Gurbax Singh was definitely able to scare Bhai Mohan Singh. Frightened, he told Gurbax Singh that he would consult his father-in-law, Bakshi Dalip Singh, who had come to Delhi for the funeral, before taking a decision.

Next day, at the meeting between the two partners, Bakshi Dalip Singh was seated next to his son-in-law. When Gurbax Singh inquired if Bhai Mohan Singh had taken a decision on his proposal, Bakshi Dalip Singh said that it would not be in Bhai Mohan Singh's best interests to pick up the Ranbaxy shares held by Gurbax Singh. Seeing his well-thought out scheme crumble before his eyes, Gurbax Singh called for a meeting of the Ranbaxy board in one final attempt to oust Bhai Mohan Singh from the company.

The die was cast. In the three-member board, the chairman's vote was crucial as whoever he supported would get full control of the company. Gurbax Singh sent Sobi-el-Ejal a message through the company secretary saying that as the chairman he should back his resolution as Bhai Mohan Singh was ignorant of the pharmaceutical business and could run the company into the ground. To Gurbax Singh's chagrin, and Bhai Mohan Singh's delight, the chairman sent a message from Mumbai a day before the board meeting, saying that there was no question of his supporting the boardroom coup. Gurbax Singh was left with no choice but to submit his resignation. He left the office in a huff in a convertible provided by Bhai Mohan Singh.

Bhai Mohan Singh wasted no time in consolidating his hold over Ranbaxy. Half an hour after Gurbax Singh had left, he dispatched a letter to the Connaught Place branch of Lloyds Bank informing it that Gurbax Singh had left the company and the authority to operate the Ranbaxy account with the bank now lay solely with Bhai Mohan Singh. Earlier, the account was being operated by both the partners.

A few months later, Gurbax Singh filed a suit in the sessions court (in those days company law matters were heard by the sessions court and not the Company Law Board) saying that he had been forcibly evicted from the Ranbaxy board and that the company should be restored to him. The resignation he had submitted earlier, Gurbax Singh told the courts, had been forcibly obtained from him.

A protracted legal battle was on the cards. However, providence intervened to help Bhai Mohan Singh. His family had done business with Lloyds Bank in Rawalpindi as well as Delhi for many years. Since he was a valued customer, the bank's top brass always treated him with courtesy and respect. Soon after Gurbax Singh had filed the case against him, Bhai Mohan Singh received a letter from the manager of the Connaught Place branch of Lloyds Bank, an Irishman by the name of Earry, asking him over for a cup of tea.

Over tea, Earry told Bhai Mohan Singh that he wanted to share some information with him. He then opened the cupboard with confidential papers in his room and took out a letter. It was from Gurbax Singh. After receiving the letter from Bhai Mohan Singh that Gurbax Singh had resigned from the company, the bank had decided to cross-check it with Gurbax Singh and had written to him, asking if the contents of Bhai Mohan Singh's letter were true. In reply, Gurbax Singh had sent a letter to the bank confirming that he had resigned from Ranbaxy. Bhai Mohan Singh knew that if he could somehow produce this letter in the courts, Gurbax Singh's plea would be thrown out in no time. But there was a hitch: Earry was not prepared to hand over the letter, as it would amount to a breach of trust. Bhai Mohan Singh was in a fix. Earry himself showed him the way out. He told Bhai Mohan Singh that he could tell the courts that he had come to know of such a letter in the possession of the bank and that the courts should summon the bank on the matter.

When the case came up for hearing next, Bhai Mohan Singh's lawyer, Prof. Veda Vyas (who was to later serve on the Ranbaxy board for many years), told the courts about the letter. Gurbax Singh knew his bluff had been called. He was left with no option but to withdraw his case. Bhai Mohan Singh had survived his first boardroom battle.

*

Gurbax Singh's descendants had lost all touch with Bhai Mohan Singh and his family. They could not be traced for their account of the corporate battle. On his part Bhai

Mohan Singh would say that this was only their first fight. Soon afterwards, Gurbax Singh fired his next salvo. One day, as Bhai Mohan Singh was in the midst of final preparations to go abroad on business, he received summons from the court of the sessions judge. Gurbax Singh had filed another case alleging that Bhai Mohan Singh had defrauded him of Rs 20,000.

It took Bhai Mohan Singh very little time to understand Gurbax Singh's ploy. A few months before Bhai Gyan Chand's death, Gurbax Singh had asked Bhai Mohan Singh for a loan of Rs 20,000. When Bhai Mohan Singh started writing him a cheque, Gurbax Singh said he needed the money that day itself because of an emergency. Bhai Mohan Singh then called for his accountant to fetch the money from the bank but found the accountant had gone out for lunch. Not wanting to disappoint his business partner, Bhai Mohan Singh gave Gurbax Singh a bearer cheque which he promptly encashed. He subsequently returned the money by cheque. Thus, while there was no proof that Bhai Mohan Singh had first given the money to Gurbax Singh, bank records would show that he had received the Rs 20,000 from Gurbax Singh.

Bhai Mohan Singh knew that this time Gurbax Singh had played his cards quite well. As he had to go abroad that very night, he scribbled 'received without plaint copy' on top of the summons and sent a copy of it to his lawyers. Meanwhile, the courts had ordered that all of Bhai Mohan Singh's bank accounts be frozen till Gurbax Singh's money was returned.

The attempt to hasten Bhai Mohan Singh's fall however undid the otherwise perfect ploy. Bhai Mohan Singh's lawyers found that on the court's copy of the summons, the last three letters of the word 'without' written by Bhai Mohan Singh had been erased. As a result, the handwritten note on top read 'received with plaint copy'. The lawyers were quick to blame Gurbax Singh for the forgery.

The judge ordered a detailed probe into the matter. Files from Bhai Mohan Singh's office were sought to verify if the note on the summons was indeed written by Bhai Mohan Singh. Once that was established, the courts called for the services of Professor Seshadri, who taught chemistry in Delhi University, to see if some letters had been erased. After carrying out various tests, Seshadri confirmed that the note had been tampered with. At this point, Gurbax Singh withdrew his case. Though it was never proved that he had a hand in the forgery, maybe he felt that his strategy was soon going to boomerang on him.

That was the last Bhai Mohan Singh and Gurbax Singh saw of each other. Gurbax Singh went on to set up a new pharmaceutical company called Gurco Pharma and died in 1967. On his part, Bhai Mohan Singh was on the road to another corporate battle, this time with Lepetit of Italy.

*

Lepetit's first dealings with Ranbaxy were in 1952, the same year that Bhai Mohan Singh joined the company. The Italian company had a product called chloramphenicol that was used in the treatment of gonorrhea, syphilis and typhoid. At that time, the incidence of typhoid was very high in India. Naturally, the Italian company was interested in the market, which was then a monopoly of Parke-Davis.

Ranbaxy was also on the lookout for a new agency at the time simply because the Japanese did not enjoy a great reputation in pharmaceuticals. They were not great innovators and, therefore, did not have a shining portfolio of products. Thus, there were limits to the extent to which Ranbaxy could grow in the market with Japanese products. Moreover, Shiniogi was known as a producer of cheap drugs. Because of its association with the Japanese company, Ranbaxy was referred to as a fifteen-anna agency. Ranbaxy salesmen were often the butt of jokes amongst chemists for the cheap drugs they sold.

At the time, Europe was the nerve centre of the global pharmaceutical business. The top companies of the world—Bayer, Hoechst, Roche, Glaxo, etc.—were all headquartered in various European countries. So Ranbaxy zeroed in on Lepetit. Italian products, especially Italian shoes and blankets, had a good reputation in India and were much sought after.

However, the Italians put a condition before signing: Ranbaxy would have to give up all the other agencies before becoming its agent. Ranbaxy could have had little objection to this caveat. Lepetit was a much bigger name than Shiniogi and the Pfizer agency (through Dey's Medical Stores) was only for north India. Ranbaxy agreed to Lepetit's condition. It opened four new offices at Kanpur, Kolkata, Mumbai and Chennai so that the new Lepetit business would grow. Soon, Lepetit's chloramphenicol, under the brand Synthomycin, was competing in the marketplace with Parke-Davis's Chloromycetin. Lepetit even gave money to Ranbaxy for advertising and publicity of the product in the country. Over a period of time, other Lepetit brands like Euromycin, Emryasynth, Petranquil and Nysone too were brought to India by Ranbaxy.

In 1956, two years after Bhai Mohan Singh had wrested control of Ranbaxy from Gurbax Singh, the government issued a new rule that the import of finished pharmaceutical products (formulations) would no longer be allowed. Instead, drugs could be imported in bulk and packaged in India. Companies like Ranbaxy, which were importing drugs from abroad, were given a year's time to take effective steps to put up a packaging facility. The government's directive was driven by its low foreign exchange reserves and the need to upgrade Indian businessmen's capabilities from trading to manufacturing.

This is how Ranbaxy's first plant at Okhla in south Delhi came up. Built in Italian style under the supervision of a Dr Franco Guzzo, a Lepetit man, the factory was completed in 1960.

*

Some time in 1959, a year before the work on the Okhla factory got completed, Bhai Mohan Singh received a letter from the Lepetit headquarters in Milan. The Italian company was now keen on having a manufacturing base for chloramphenicol in India in collaboration with Bhai Mohan Singh. Indian government rules at that time did not permit foreign pharmaceutical companies to set up shop in the country on their own. They could only come into India as a minority partner in a joint venture with an Indian company. The letter asked Bhai Mohan Singh to come to Milan immediately for further negotiations on the matter.

Lepetit's choice of Bhai Mohan Singh as its partner in the Indian venture could have been driven by several facts. One, it had had a relationship with him for many years. Two, he had the financial resources to bring his share of funds to the venture. Finally, he was very well connected in Delhi's corridors of power. In a highly regulated business environment, this last factor was crucial. The worth of any businessman could be judged not only by his bank balance but also the number of secretaries to various ministries he knew.

Though he was excited at the prospect of forming a manufacturing joint venture with Lepetit, Bhai Mohan Singh was unwell when he received the letter. So he replied saying that he would not be able to come. But the Italians were persistent and suggested he bring his wife, Avtar Kaur, along to look after him in Milan. Soon, the couple was on their way to Milan. After discussing the matter with the Lepetit brass for nearly a week, Bhai Mohan Singh travelled with the company's top-ranking executives to London to sign a memorandum of understanding. Lepetit agreed to ship a chloramphenicol plant to India, which was to be set up in a building adjacent to the Okhla factory.

From the beginning, Lepetit was clear that it would run the Indian venture, exercising total control. After all, it was giving the technology for the venture. Besides, Bhai Mohan

Singh had no experience of running a manufacturing outfit. Looking at the benefits of a plant in India, which would have brought down the cost of the Lepetit chloramphenicol in the country substantially, he agreed to give control of the company to his Italian partners.

However, there was the small matter of government rules under which the Italians could, at best, acquire a 49 per cent stake. The Italians found a way out—while they would hold a 45 per cent stake in the company, an Indian investor of their choice would hold another 6 per cent. Thus, they would have effective control of the company, without violating any rules. Lepetit chose a Mumbai-based Gujarati financier, Kishore Prem Chand, as the 'friendly' 6 per cent-investor. Thus, Lepetit Ranbaxy Ltd was born with Bhai Mohan Singh controlling 49 per cent of the shareholding (40 per cent directly and 9 per cent through friends and associates) and Lepetit the remaining 51 per cent (45 per cent directly and 6 per cent through Kishore Prem Chand).

The Italians had a majority on the company's board of directors and control of the management. Out of the five directors on the board, two—Dr Carnalori and Braham Shah, an Egyptian of Lebanese origin who had earlier been the Lepetit agent in Egypt—were nominated by Lepetit, two—Bhai Mohan Singh himself and J.C. Jain, a friend of his—were Ranbaxy's representatives and the fifth director was Kishore Prem Chand. Bhai Mohan Singh was the chairman and general manager of Lepetit Ranbaxy; Shah and Carnalori were both deputy general managers.

*

Unfortunately, the joint venture died an early death. In a few short years, Lapetit was out and Bhai Mohan Singh had gained control of the company. No records were kept of Lapetit's version of what went wrong. What follows is the sequence of events according to Bhai Mohan Singh and his friends. Though the joint venture company had been formed in 1959, there was no sign of the chloramphenicol plant for the next three years. Lepetit had shipped a machine to India which was never put to use. Meanwhile, the company continued to import the drug in bulk from Italy and package it into capsules, tablets and later also syrups.

The company went into the red in 1959 itself. This was particularly painful for Bhai Mohan Singh. He was an indulgent employer and would regularly pay his employees an annual bonus of three months' salary. He was getting restive and he put the blame for the losses on the handful of Italian expatriates working in the company. Being expatriates, they received very high salaries. The company had to rent expensive houses in upscale residential colonies for them and also bear their travel expenses within India and to Italy.

There was only one way out for Bhai Mohan Singh. It had to be brought to the notice of the Indian government that three years after it had promised to bring a chloramphenicol plant to India, Lepetit had not done so. If Bhai Mohan Singh himself were to lodge the complaint, it would be a tremendous loss of face for him. After all, it was he who had lobbied hard with the government to let the Italians in.

The friends and associates of Bhai Mohan Singh, who together held a 9 per cent stake in the company, came in handy. They wrote to the government, informing it of the state of affairs. The government was quick to react. The early-1960s had seen a serious outbreak of typhoid and the government did not take kindly to Lepetit Ranbaxy's inability to put up a chloramphenicol plant. A notice to this effect was promptly issued to the company. But no satisfactory answer was forthcoming.

The government reacted by appointing two directors on the Lepetit Ranbaxy board. While one was the Drug Controller of India, the other was a representative of the

Company Law Board, R.M. Bhandari. The brief of the two officials was to find out why the company had failed to implement the project.

Meanwhile, Kishore Prem Chand had shifted from Mumbai to Switzerland. Bhai Mohan Singh saw this as an opportunity to cut him off from the board. He sent a terse letter saying that since his address in the company's record was in Mumbai, the company could only send an air ticket to and from Mumbai, and not Switzerland.

Soon, a meeting of the Lepetit Ranbaxy board was called, where the Lepetit directors were hopelessly outnumbered because Kishore Prem Chand was stranded in Switzerland. The meeting began at ten in the morning and heated arguments continued till six in the evening. The Lepetit directors were grilled by the other board members and they finally asked for one week's time to go to Milan for consultations and come back with a final word. Their request was accepted. When the board met a week later, the Lepetit directors still did not have a satisfactory answer.

The government directors then lay their cards on the table: either the Italian company should furnish a bank guarantee of Rs 1 crore that it would put up a plant or it would have to leave the country. After protracted consultations with their headquarters in Milan, the directors said that Lepetit was willing to give any guarantee, except a financial one, that it would put up the plant. Wary of the Italian company's promises, the government said this was unacceptable and, in 1964, it asked Lepetit to leave India.

Lepetit had reached a dead end. In a way, it had made the same mistake as Gurbax Singh had in underestimating Bhai Mohan Singh's ability to rally support from the quarters that mattered. Such examples of a bigger partner being worsted by the smaller partner in a corporate battle are rare in India's corporate history. Even more rare are instances of a foreign company being outwitted by its Indian partner.

The Italian company agreed to exit the Indian joint venture company if Bhai Mohan Singh agreed to pick up its shares within three months. While showing his willingness to do so, Bhai Mohan Singh had another problem to sort out. If he snapped his ties with Lepetit, he would be left with no products to market. So he told Lepetit that he would buy its block of shares only if he was given the licence to use Lepetit brands in the Indian market for another five years. During this period, he thought he would be able to replace the Lepetit brands with his own brands.

Cornered by the affable, mild-mannered Sikh, Lepetit agreed to the condition. Bhai Mohan Singh offered to pick up the shares at par. The total consideration worked out to Rs 25 lakh. Lepetit agreed and asked Bhai Mohan Singh to deposit the money in Citibank and take the delivery of the shares. Partly by dipping into his personal kitty and partly by recalling the loans he had given (he was still carrying on his financier's business), Bhai Mohan Singh put together the required sum and took over the shares. Lepetit Ranbaxy became Ranbaxy Laboratories Ltd, owned fully by Bhai Mohan Singh.

Why did Lepetit not put up the plant? Decades later, there are still no clear-cut answers. One reason could be that the patent for chloramphenicol was held by Parke-Davis. As India recognized product patents at that time, Lepetit would have to obtain permission from Parke-Davis before beginning production in India. Since Parke-Davis was the leader in the chloramphenicol market in India, which was one of the biggest markets for the drug at that time, it would not have been in its best interests to allow a rival to produce the drug. It is possible that Parke-Davis would have agreed to give its permission if Lepetit agreed to pay an exorbitant sum as royalty, which would have made the Indian venture commercially unviable.

Instead of the five years' time that he had sought, Bhai Mohan Singh was able to replace the Lepetit brands with his own brands—Renphenicol in place of Synthomycin, Ranacycline for Euromycin, Cyclocetin for Emryasynth, Ranquil for Petranquil and Ranbisolone for Nysone—in just two years. However, none of these products were to fetch great success for Ranbaxy. For that it had to wait till 1968, when it launched its first blockbuster, Calmpose.

3

India's First Superbrand

Situated on the banks of the river Rhine, Basel is a busy little town in northern Switzerland, on its border with France and Germany. It was here, on 1 October 1896, that a man named Fritz Hoffmann-La Roche founded F. Hoffmann-La Roche & Co., a drug company that would, over the next few decades, spread its wings all over the world.

Roche was founded at a time when Europe was making rapid advances in the social and scientific arenas, and this extended to medicine as well. Drug companies all over Europe were now considering large-scale production of medicine to supply the whole world and Fritz Hoffman-La Roche shared this dream.

Though the company had come out with a preparation for thyroid disorders and a cough syrup by 1896, its first big success came two years later, in 1898, when it introduced Sirolin, a non-prescription cough syrup using Roche's own thiocol as its active ingredient. The syrup's orange flavour made it an immediate success. Sirolin went on to stay in the market for no less than sixty years.

Roche decided early on to focus on pain and anxiety relief. In 1909, it came out with Pantopon, a remedy for pain, colic, spasms and cough. Pantopon is still sold in a few countries, making it Roche's longest-selling product. In 1921, Roche introduced Allonal, an analgesic sedative and hypnotic (sleep-inducer). This was the first product which used compounds produced by synthetic chemistry. In 1938, it came out with another analgesic called Saridon, which is still a household name in many countries, including India.

Roche had earned a name for itself as one of the world's leading players in vitamins by the mid-1940s. In the 1950s, its research diversified into a number of areas ranging from antidepressants and anti-microbials to agents for cancer chemotherapy and inflammatory and cardiovascular diseases. But everything was to be eclipsed by the sensational development in the field of tranquillizers. Roche scientists, led by Nobel laureate Leo Sternbach, had stumbled upon the benzodiazepine molecule, which proved to be the base for many milestone drugs in the years to come. Librium, the first of the class of benzodiazepine, was launched in 1960 as a cure for emotional, psychosomatic and muscular disorders.

Librium proved to be a runaway success for Roche and the company decided to come out with more drugs from the benzodiazepine family. Thus, it launched diazepam under the brand name Valium in 1963. This was by far the best tranquillizer the world had ever seen. It turned out to be an instant success and established Roche's worldwide reputation in psychotropic medications.

*

Once Lepetit had exited from Ranbaxy in 1961, Bhai Mohan Singh had to quickly think of new products, though he had managed to turn the company around—by 1964, Ranbaxy had notched up a profit of Rs 2.96 lakh. Ranbaxy had in its portfolio a tranquillizer called Ranquil, its version of Petranquil that it had inherited from Lepetit. Bhai Mohan Singh was aware that Roche's diazepam was an improvement over this drug; while Ranquil came in a 500 mg tablet, a Valium tablet weighed just 5 mg.

India did not figure in Roche's gameplan for Valium, though it had introduced Librium in the country. But Valium was at least a generation ahead. Most multinational pharmaceutical companies at that time chose to bring a product to India only after it had been sufficiently flogged in the West and had reached the end of its life cycle. Roche was no different. Least expecting an Indian company to come out with a clone, Roche had not registered a patent for Valium in India. Bhai Mohan Singh began to think of ways to get the drug to India.

The communist bloc countries had rejected the idea of patents and many of these countries freely made patented medicines. There was little that pharmaceutical companies could do about it. India was close to the Soviet Union and its allies at that time. Realizing that there was a possibility of sourcing diazepam from one of these countries, Bhai Mohan Singh wrote to almost twenty communist countries asking them to sell diazepam to him. A state-owned firm in Hungary finally agreed, and Bhai Mohan Singh was able to procure diazepam in 1968. The bulk drug would be shipped to Ranbaxy's Okhla factory where it would be converted into formulations, packaged and sold. While Roche was selling its diazepam at $12,000 per kg, Ranbaxy's diazepam would cost only Rs 3,000 per kg, which included an import duty of 120 per cent. (The dollar was hovering between Rs 7 and Rs 8 at the time.) The next task at hand was to find a brand name for the product and market it.

*

Help came from two persons—Sorab Desai and Narinder Singh Sawhney.

Sorab Desai was an Indian scientist who had been working at the University of Michigan, Ann Arbor, where he had got to know Bhai Mohan Singh's eldest son, Parvinder, who was studying there, quite well. Desai joined Ranbaxy in 1968 only to leave soon after in order to pursue an academic career in the United States. During his short tenure, he gave Ranbaxy its brand name for diazepam—Calmpose, India's first pharmaceutical superbrand. Parvinder remained close to Desai for the rest of his life.

Sawhney, a Sikh from Rawalpindi with an artistic bent of mind, was the head of marketing at Ranbaxy at the time. Though he had no background of medicine, he was an effective communicator and he was given the task of writing the literature for the drug, which Ranbaxy's representatives would pass on to doctors.

Sawhney was actually 'acquired' by Ranbaxy. He had been working for a Kanpur-based medicine dealership owned by Bhai Mohan Singh's college friend, S.S. Charai. Once Bhai Mohan Singh got full control of Ranbaxy, Charai's trading business was merged into it. Bhai Mohan Singh had known Sawhney's father in Rawalpindi and would affectionately call him Nandu. Sawhney, who was of medium height and slightly corpulent, for his part, was fiercely loyal to his employer.

Sawhney kicked off the marketing campaign with a poster bearing a couplet composed by Ghalib, the legendary nineteenth-century poet: '*Maut ka ek din muaiyan hai; neend raat bhar kyon aati nahin* (when the day of death is set, why does sleep elude me all night)'. The campaign was a runaway success, especially in north India. Doctors continued to display the poster for years. However, it did not make much headway in the South where people were less familiar with Ghalib. Ranbaxy also played up one of the side effects of Librium, obesity, when it began marketing its own diazepam. The virgin diazepam market was totally conquered by Ranbaxy.

This was perhaps the first instance in India when a company's brand came to be better known than the company. In the medical fraternity, Ranbaxy began to be known as the company which made Calmpose, just as Vadodara-based Alembic was known as the company which made Glycodin cough syrup.

At that time, the multinational pharmaceutical companies like Pfizer, Glaxo, Abbott Laboratories, Sandoz and Ceiba had a stranglehold over the Indian market. Their products enjoyed a very good reputation and doctors were not willing to touch drugs made by Indian companies. This was particularly true of the top-drawer doctors, who set the trend by prescribing a brand first. With Calmpose, Ranbaxy was able to break through this psychological barrier, though it would take many more years before its other drugs could get the same level of acceptability. Doctors would tell Ranbaxy medical representatives to stick to Calmpose whenever they tried to sell other products.

Money now started flowing into Ranbaxy's coffers. In 1969, the company first recorded a sales turnover in excess of Rs 1 crore. Turnover, in fact, jumped that year by over 25 per cent as Ranbaxy launched its diazepam and ampicillin (under the trade name Roscillin) in the market. The directors' report to the company's shareholders noted that these two drugs 'helped in improving the image of the company in pharmaceutical circles'.

Meanwhile, there were newspaper reports that the government was mulling a price control on drugs in order to make medicines affordable and available to all, especially the poor. More than anything else, this threatened to erode Ranbaxy's newfound profitability after it had launched Calmpose. The fears were reflected in the 1969 directors' report:

> It is apprehended that this would have an adverse affect on the progress and development of most pharmaceutical companies and industry in general.

However, since our products are already reasonably priced, this might not affect us as badly as some other foreign companies whose prices are very high.

The reference to the high cost of Roche's Valium is unmistakable. Roche finally launched Valium in India in 1974. But it was too late by then.

Over the years, Calmpose became a generic name for antidepressants. People would buy it over the counter from chemists rather than wait for the physician's prescription. Ultimately, this worked against the brand. When doctors started prescribing Valium, Calmpose sales fell. Its sagging fortunes could be revived only in the mid-1980s.

*

This was also the period when Parvinder, Bhai Mohan Singh's favourite son, joined the family business. Bhai Mohan Singh had been quick to fill key vacancies in his company with close relatives and friends. Four months after he took over Ranbaxy in August 1952, his brother-in-law, Jaswant Singh, joined the company. Sawhney came on board on 9 April 1954 and Man Singh Kohli on 1 November 1955. Yet, in a sense it was a lonesome vigil for Bhai Mohan Singh, till Parvinder joined the company on 10 December 1967.

However, this was not Parvinder's first exposure to Ranbaxy. He had been co-opted as a director on the Ranbaxy board in 1965, along with Veda Vyas. Apart from Bhai Mohan Singh, his close friends J.C. Jain and Dan Singh Bawa were already on the board. The next year, his wife, Avtar Mohan Singh (better known as Avtar Kaur), joined the board as an alternate director to Parvinder. In 1967, Parvinder left the board, while Avtar Mohan Singh became an additional director.

*

When he moved to Delhi after Partition, Bhai Mohan Singh sent Parvinder to the Doon School at Dehradun, where the children of the rich and famous of India went to study. Parvinder's schoolmates included the sons of leading businessmen like Dr Bharat Ram of Delhi Cloth Mills Ltd (changed to DCM Ltd in the mid-1980s) and H.P. Nanda of Escorts, to name just two.

Though he was not a brilliant student, Parvinder made a mark in sports, particularly athletics, hockey, squash and tennis. Later in life, he became an avid golfer and was credited with having the longest drive in the whole country. People who played with him regularly often felt that he could have become India's top golfer, if only he had the time.

After completing school, Parvinder enrolled in St. Stephen's College in Delhi for a graduation course in chemistry. Though he continued to be a fun-loving person and prankster—his friend Surendra 'Mickey' Daulat Singh, who was staying in the hostel, would often find a dissected lizard on his doorknob—it was here that he excelled in studies and stood first in his class. Instead of joining the family business, Parvinder said he wanted to study further. Bhai Mohan Singh readily agreed and wrote to four universities in the United States. Parvinder got admission in a university in California. After graduating from there he expressed his desire to go to the University of Michigan, Ann Arbor, for a doctoral degree. Bhai Mohan Singh gave his nod and Parvinder enrolled in the university on a stipend of $300 per month.

Here, Parvinder shared a flat with his old friends, Arun Bharat Ram and Vivek Bharat Ram. While the Bharat Ram brothers enjoyed themselves, Parvinder buried himself in his work. He would reach the laboratory at eight in the morning and would seldom be back before ten at night. Often, the only light on in the laboratory at midnight would be Parvinder's. Yet he did not avoid socializing entirely.

Photographs taken by the Bharat Ram brothers those days show Parvinder to be both fun loving and outgoing. During summer, the three friends would play golf. He would occasionally eat non-vegetarian food and take a drink or two. (He was to give it all up for the rest of his life soon after.) He was also particular about his attire and would seldom be seen without a tie and a jacket.

Though they were scions of India's richest families, they still had to fend for themselves. While Vivek did not like doing the dishes, Parvinder had no particular interest in cooking. So while Vivek would prepare the meals, Parvinder would diligently clean all the dishes. The problem was Vivek knew how to make only one dish. Parvinder could not be blamed, when one day, after a year of eating the same food, he threw the food out of the window.

At the University of Michigan, Ann Arbor, Parvinder got his degree in just two years. From Parvinder, he became Dr Singh. The dean of the university wrote to Bhai Mohan Singh that a student like his son came to the university only once in ten years.

More importantly, Parvinder's business vision was evolving during his days in the United States. 'Even in the United States, I could see that Parvinder would one day change Ranbaxy, which was, at that time, a me-too company. Though I didn't know that he would one day take over the reins of the company, but I was certain he would change the destiny of the company. I could sense that without any doubt. He would say how backward we were in our thinking, oriented towards licensing and copying,' Arun Bharat Ram would recall after the death of his friend in 1997.

In December 1967, Dr Singh returned to India. Within forty-eight hours of touching down in Delhi, he had joined Ranbaxy.

*

Soon after his return, Dr Singh's mother started worrying about his marriage. Since he was spending the whole day at Ranbaxy's Okhla office, she found it difficult to talk to him. After waiting for a few months, she asked Bhai Mohan Singh to take Dr Singh out for lunch and convince him to get married. But Dr Singh stonewalled all attempts by his parents to get him to marry.

The Bharat Ram brothers were also back in India and the three would meet frequently. While Dr Singh continued to be fun loving and full of life, there were definite signs of change in him. He had become very sensitive and focussed, and was developing a philosophical bent of mind. This was not a sudden development. During his last days in the United States, he had become a follower of a Canadian female guru, but had moved away soon after. His quest for spiritual fulfilment was not lost on the people around him, least of all on Sheila Bharat Ram, the mother of Arun and Vivek.

Sheila Bharat Ram happened to be a follower of the Radhasoami Satsang spiritual movement and was close to the leader of the faith, Gurcharan Singh, who everybody referred to as Maharaj Ji. Whenever in Delhi, the Maharaj Ji used to stay with the Bharat Rams in Lal Kothi, their sprawling house on Kitchener Road (now Sardar Patel Marg). One day, she asked Dr Singh to meet Nirmaljit (Nimmi), Maharaj Ji's daughter. Having embarked on his journey for spiritual discovery, Dr Singh agreed and the two first met at Dr Bharat Ram's Chhattarpur farmhouse in south Delhi. The two hit it off well and it was decided to take the matter up with the parents.

Bhai Mohan Singh and his wife took an instant liking to Nimmi. She had studied in a convent in Dalhousie and carried herself with grace and dignity. Bhai Mohan Singh and his wife then travelled to Beas to finalize the arrangements. However, Bhai Mohan Singh was a little perplexed when he did not find a copy of the Guru Granth

Sahib, the holy book of the Sikhs, within the Satsang complex at Beas. He then put the condition that the marriage would take place according to Sikh rites, which the Maharaj Ji agreed to.

Dr Singh's marriage took place at Beas in 1970. The wedding itself was simple. But Bhai Mohan Singh booked an entire train to take his guests to Beas. Cooks were sent in advance to Karnal, which was on the route to Beas, where food and drinks were served to the guests. The empty bottles were offloaded at Ludhiana before the train reached Beas. The other guests who wanted to continue with their drinks and revelry were put up at the guesthouse of Jagatjit Industries—owned by Bhai Mohan Singh's friend, Ladli Prasad Jayaswal—at Hamira near Beas.

*

Soon after Dr Singh joined Ranbaxy, a development took place which would change the Indian pharmaceutical scene dramatically. At the time of Independence, India had inherited a product patents regime from the British. The government set up the Bakshi Tekchand Committee in the 1950s to see if the Patent Act, 1930, needed to be changed. However, this committee failed to come up with any concrete proposals. Meanwhile, homegrown pharmaceutical companies like Cipla and Mumbai-based Unichem Laboratories had started demanding a change in the law since they found all their proposals to make new medicines being blocked by one patent or the other. As a result, they could make only old medicines, which had gone off-patent. However, with rapid advances being made in the field of medicine the world over, making old medicines was no longer commercially viable. Besides, this also meant that Indian drug companies could not grow beyond a certain size.

This was the time when the government was encouraging self-reliance in all sectors of industry, and Prime Minister

Jawaharlal Nehru was keen that a vibrant pharmaceutical sector develop in the country. His government had set up two public sector units, Hindustan Antibiotics Ltd to make penicillin and Indian Drugs and Pharmaceuticals Ltd (IDPL) to make off-patent bulk drugs. The government was under tremendous pressure from the multinational pharmaceutical companies not to change the patent law. As the country was dependent on these companies for health-care services, it could ill-afford to ignore them. Naturally, drug prices in India at that time were amongst the highest in the world.

In the early 1960s, the government set up the R.S. Iyengar Committee to trace the development of patent systems all over the world, especially in developing countries. This committee observed that patent laws in any country need to be linked to its state of technological development. It also stated emphatically that patent laws should not be used to create a monopoly. Though scientific effort needs some protection, this could not be at the cost of the people. This led to a prolonged public debate with the majority favouring a change in the patent legislation.

Yet the government continued to hesitate till 1970, when Indira Gandhi, Jawaharlal Nehru's pugnacious daughter, took the bull by the horns and decided to change the Patent Act. The new Patent Act, 1970, replaced product patents with process patents. In other words, an Indian pharmaceutical company could make any drug in the world so long as it did not violate a patented process. This was expected to set off a flowering of the Indian pharmaceutical industry. The first to make the most of the new Patent Act was Ranbaxy.

*

By 1971, within two years of the launch of Calmpose, Ranbaxy had started reporting very healthy profits, enough to start looking beyond the immediate future. The annual report of 1971 first indicated that the company would up research and development work on its own. It made a beginning by sponsoring basic research of four pharmaceutical chemicals through the National Research Laboratories of the Council for Scientific and Industrial Research (CSIR). The directors' report noted that 'efforts are being made to enlarge the set-up of research facilities within the company, for which senior officers having experience in research abroad have been selected'. There was also a hint that the company would get into the production of bulk drugs soon.

The robust turnover growth continued into 1972, with the company reporting a turnover of Rs 2.39 crore and a net profit of Rs 22.91 lakh for the year. This was propelled by Calmpose, which occupied the pride of place in a picture of the company's products on the first page of the 1972 annual report. Roscillin was nowhere in the picture, the company having discontinued its production because of the high cost of imported ampicillin.

With the patent legislation opening up new opportunities, and with ample cash in its coffers, Ranbaxy rethought its strategy. The business model followed so far—that of importing medicine—was unsustainable in the long run, though it could still be pursued with the change in the Patent Act. A strategy of importing a patented drug from a country which did not recognize patents, as was done in the case of diazepam, could be followed in the future as well. However, it was unlikely that Ranbaxy would be able to lay its hands on a blockbuster medicine by following this route. Besides, such an arrangement required no technical or scientific skills; others could play the game too.

Moreover, the company was considering diversifying into antibiotics. Though it had the lion's share of the diazepam market in the country, the antidepressants market was not a large one. The profile of the pharmaceutical market of a country depends on the state of its socio-economic development. Anti-infective drugs will dominate the market of underdeveloped countries, while the market in developed countries would be tilted towards lifestyle therapies like those for cardiovascular ailments, and anxiety and depression. India was still at the lower end of the socio-economic scale in the early 1970s, and was coping with various epidemics. The demand for anti-infective drugs, especially penicillin derivatives, was high. The message for Ranbaxy was clear: if it harboured any ambition of being a large pharmaceutical company, it would have to grow beyond diazepam.

Dr Singh had been looking for a window of opportunity ever since his return from the United States. Having seen the pharmaceutical industry at work there, he was convinced that it was necessary for Ranbaxy to invest in research and development, as well as in manufacturing if it had to survive in the long run. The Patent Act, 1970, offered him this window. With the new process patent regime in place, the company could make it big by mastering process technologies. For that, it would need to invest in a research and development outfit. It also had to set up a manufacturing unit to put new process technologies to commercial use. This would also give the company total control over the quality of the medicine it sold, which it could not ensure when it imported drugs. The control over quality was particularly important if it wanted to export its products.

In 1972, the company had been allotted an industrial plot for producing bulk drugs in the industrial township of Mohali near Chandigarh. By now, the company had also finalized its vision for research and development. The 1972 directors' report noted:

> 'In order to enlarge our product range and reduce our dependence on the import of know-how and products by being able to develop the same ourselves and manufacture the essential drugs in the country, . . . (the) company . . . has now established a full-

> fledged R&D laboratory equipped with modern sophisticated equipment under the supervision of a highly qualified and experienced staff.'

This laboratory was at the Okhla plant. Ranbaxy went in for a public issue in 1973 to bankroll the project and raised Rs 70 lakh from the market. Its initial public offer was oversubscribed fourteen times. The Controller of Capital Issues (an office now scrapped) decreed that the company make allotments in lots of fifty instead of the prescribed 100 in view of the interest shown by the investors.

The same year the government reduced diazepam prices and the Reserve Bank of India enforced a credit squeeze, as there was a shortage of foreign exchange in the country. This only reinforced Dr Singh's belief in backward integration into bulk drugs. The uncertainty over the prices and availability of imported bulk drugs, coupled with the arbitrary price fixation by the government, meant there was only one way a pharmaceutical company could survive—total control over its raw material by producing bulk drugs.

By 1974, Ranbaxy's Mohali plant making diazepam with CSIR technology was ready. Bhai Mohan Singh played another masterstroke at this point. Using the pretext of protection for CSIR, he lobbied with the government to get the import of diazepam banned. This gave him a virtual monopoly in the market, with even Roche buying diazepam from Ranbaxy for the Indian market! But the monopoly did not last for very long. By then, the public sector IDPL had also started producing diazepam. In addition, a number of smaller companies would start importing diazepam intermediates, which was not banned, convert the bulk drugs into formulations and sell these in the market.

*

The 1973 public issue saw the first wave of professionals joining the company. Till then, key posts had been filled by

Bhai Mohan Singh's relatives. There were almost thirty of them on the company's rolls at that time. Kishan Jit Singh Chowdhury, the estates manager, was related to Avtar Kaur. Jaswant Singh, Bhai Mohan Singh's brother-in-law, was in charge of accounts. While Dr Singh was looking after operations, the second son, Bhai Manjit Singh, who had joined the company on 10 October 1968, was responsible for purchases. A second cousin of Avtar Kaur was the chief timekeeper at the Okhla factory. The storekeeper came from the same village as Bhai Mohan Singh.

The America-returned Dr Singh would often tell his close friends how the company was being run without professionals. But he was too new to effect top-level changes. Meanwhile, Ranbaxy was under pressure from its bankers to induct professionals. This was also expected to improve the company's prospects in the primary market. Their pressure provided Dr Singh the opening he needed to induct fresh blood into the company. He had his father's full support.

The first professional to be recruited was P.D. Sheth, who was working for ICI in the United States. Sheth spent the rest of his working life with Ranbaxy, rising to serve on the company's board of directors. A non-resident Indian, he gave up his permanent residence visa to the United States.

The next person to come aboard was K.W. Gopinath, a scientist of repute from the Regional Research Laboratory (RRL) of the CSIR at Jorhat in Assam. He was put in charge of the company's small research and development team, which was expected to develop process technologies. Gopinath soon proved his worth by stabilizing the CSIR technology used by Ranbaxy at its Mohali plant to make diazepam after it had exhibited some initial problems. Then came Bimal Raizada, the first professional to look after the company's finances. He took over the function from Jaswant Singh.

Raizada came from a family of lawyers, with one of his

ancestors having come to Delhi in 1702 to become the chief *munsif* (equivalent to a high court judge) of Emperor Aurangzeb. His father was a public prosecutor at the time of Partition. But he felt that the prospects for a newcomer in the legal profession were not very bright and he persuaded his sons to break the family tradition and choose a new career. After studying chartered accountancy from London, Raizada signed up with an audit firm called Bass Charington. But he found the audit profession boring and started looking for opportunities. When there was an opening in the American pharmaceutical firm Warner-Lambert, a client of Bass Charington, Raizada grabbed it. Warner-Lambert posted him to Mumbai as a systems and audit manager.

Working for Warner-Lambert was a dream come true for any young executive. The company traced its history to 1856, when William R. Warner launched his own chemist shop in Philadelphia, Pennsylvania. He had invented a tablet-coating process to encase bitter-tasting medicines in sugar shells. This innovation earned Warner a place in the Smithsonian Institution. In 1886, Warner gave up his retail shop and focussed solely on drug manufacturing under the name William R. Warner & Co. In 1908, the company was bought by a St. Louis-based company, Pfeiffer Chemical, which retained the Warner name. The company grew through acquisitions, one of which was another St. Louis-based company, Lambert Pharmacal, whose main product was the antiseptic, Listerine. In 1955, the Warner-Lambert Pharmaceutical Company came into existence. Warner-Lambert also took the acquisitions route to grow. In 1970 came the deal that transformed Warner-Lambert: the acquisition of Parke-Davis, once the world's largest drugmaker. Warner-Lambert continued the acquisition spree till 2000 when it got merged into Pfizer, making the latter the world's largest pharmaceutical company. Only a fool would think of leaving such a company.

Citibank had contacted Raizada in early 1972. The

bank had been engaged by Ranbaxy, even then a little known Delhi-based pharmaceutical company, which wanted to professionalize its finance department. There wasn't much in the deal. While Warner-Lambert was amongst the top ten players in the Indian pharmaceutical market, Ranbaxy was placed a distant forty. Yet, he decided to give it a shot.

Raizada was first interviewed by Ranbaxy executive director S.P. Jain, an Indian Administrative Service (IAS) officer from the Punjab cadre and a close friend of Bhai Mohan Singh. Raizada then met Dr Singh, who struck him as a classical technocrat but a highly impatient person. He was openly critical of the way Ranbaxy was functioning, especially of its internal systems, and wanted to make changes in double quick time. He was completely open to let an outsider get a view of his money—Ranbaxy was still a closely held company at that time. Finally, Raizada was interviewed by Bhai Mohan Singh, who promised him a completely free hand.

Raizada told Jain that he was willing to join provided he was offered a 20 per cent increase in salary. Jain refused to commit himself but wrote to Raizada a few days later, offering him the raise he had asked for. Raizada packed his bags and shifted from Mumbai to Delhi.

Raizada got to know the real story behind his recruitment much later. Ranbaxy was changing from banking with Indian banks like Union Bank and Punjab National Bank to foreign banks like Citibank. So it needed somebody in charge of finance whom Citibank would be comfortable with. Indeed, Raizada found that the company had a very rudimentary accounting system, which was more of a mere recording of expenses and income than analysis. This system needed an overhaul if Ranbaxy were to do business with Citibank. Besides, the public offer was around the corner and Ranbaxy needed to present as professional a face as possible to investors.

It also slowly dawned on Raizada that he was not

completely unknown at Ranbaxy. On his first day at work, Bhai Mohan Singh's friend, Meherban Singh Dhupia, came to welcome him. Dhupia's son was Raizada's school friend. He also came to know that Bhai Mohan Singh was very friendly with his uncle, K.B. Lall, the then Union Commerce Secretary. Board member J.C. Jain knew Raizada's father very well. A month after he had joined, Bhai Mohan Singh threw a party at his house to introduce him to his business associates. To his utter surprise, Raizada met a number of his relatives there. Bhai Mohan Singh had got a thorough check done on Raizada before appointing him. Without knowing it, Raizada was an insider. Ranbaxy was not sharing its finances with a rank outsider.

A little before Sheth, Gopinath and Raizada came on board, Ranbaxy had recruited S.K. Chakroborty for its Chennai office. Over the next few years, Chakroborty was to rise quickly through the ranks and succeed Sawhney when he retired in 1984. He was the genius behind Ranbaxy's innumerable success stories, including the second innings of Calmpose.

Born at Pabna in north Bengal (now in Bangladesh), Chakroborty was brought up in Kolkata. After finishing college, he aspired to be a journalist and enrolled in Lake College for a course in journalism. But even while he was doing the course, it was apparent to Chakroborty that there were not many avenues in journalism, and whatever jobs were there did not pay well.

Disenchanted, Chakroborty joined Glaxo as a sales representative in 1958. At that time, Glaxo was a very large company with a big office in Kolkata, where some of the top functionaries were British. Though it did not have a blockbuster drug in its portfolio, the company was well known for its products like vitamins, tonics and, above all, Farex baby food. Chakroborty was first posted to Ranchi, then in south Bihar and now the capital of Jharkhand. He worked in Glaxo for three years, observing carefully how the sales function of the company was organized. It taught him how a company with ordinary products could create tremendous brand loyalty.

From Glaxo, Chakroborty moved to another multinational, the United States-based Merck, Sharp and Dhome in 1961. A very conservative and high-nosed company, Merck, Sharp and Dhome was amongst the late entrants to India, having come here only in 1960. With two Nobel laureates working for it, its entry created excitement and a lot of young people from other pharmaceutical companies, including Chakroborty, joined it.

Merck, Sharp and Dhome laid a lot of emphasis on the training of its sales force. The company's medical representatives were taught not only the scientific aspects of medicine but also speechmaking and diction. The entire promotional literature was prepared at the company's headquarters in New Jersey and medical representatives had to memorize it. Chakroborty had a photographic memory and could memorize the text at a glance, while others would take a day or more to do it. This impressed his bosses and the company promoted him and transferred him from Kolkata to Mumbai as the manager for the city and half of Maharashtra.

In 1964, Chakroborty got married and needed a bigger house, something he could afford only if it was in the faraway suburbs of Mumbai. Chakroborty then got an offer from Tata Fison, a joint venture between the Mumbai-based House of Tatas and British diversified firm Fison. A company flat was part of the remuneration package. Chakroborty grabbed the offer and joined Tata Fison in 1966.

Fison had an array of businesses ranging from leather to pesticides, agricultural inputs and pharmaceuticals. Its main pharmaceutical product was the Inferon injection to build up intra-muscular iron. The injection was better than an oral administration because it cured iron deficiency in a week and had no side effects. Iron deficiency among women was and continues to be a common problem in India and is the cause of maternal deaths. At Tata Fison, Chakroborty had to deal with all the hospitals, mostly with gynaecologists.

From Tata Fison, Chakroborty moved briefly to Searle. But things did not work out and Chakroborty was once again looking for a job. He had applied to Sandoz and also had an offer from Abbott. But he was aware that multinationals rarely take outsiders in middle and top management positions, preferring to promote people within the company. Moreover, Abbott wanted him to stay in Mumbai, which Chakroborty was a little reluctant to do.

In-between all this, Chakroborty had been interviewed by Bhai Mohan Singh in the rundown Ranbaxy office in Kolkata near the city's wholesale market for medicine. The first impression on Chakroborty, who had so far worked only with multinational companies, was disturbing. The company had no products and no production facility. The meeting did nothing to lift Chakroborty's sagging spirits, though he developed an instant respect for Bhai Mohan Singh. The tall and handsome Sikh, wearing a big turban, had an aristocratic bearing with very pleasant manners.

After the interview, Bhai Mohan Singh offered to make Chakroborty Ranbaxy's branch manager in Chennai. Though Chakroborty was in desperate need for a job, he was not sure if he should take up the offer. At that point, his father intervened and told his son that Sikhs are good people and he should work with Bhai Mohan Singh. In June 1970, Chakroborty joined Ranbaxy as the Chennai branch manager reporting to Sawhney. It proved to be the turning point in his life. By 1975, Chakroborty had moved to Delhi to become a part of Ranbaxy's core marketing team.

*

By the early-1980s, it had come to Ranbaxy's notice that the prescription base for diazepam was shifting from

Calmpose to Valium. However, there was still value to be derived from the brand.

Ranbaxy had come out with an injectible Calmpose in 1972, which was popular amongst doctors for controlling short and localized pain during surgeries. Chakroborty hit upon the idea of marketing Calmpose and Fortwin (which had by now replaced morphine) together to take care of anxiety as well as pain during surgeries. He devised a special campaign, with new visuals and new detailing literature, targeted at surgeons and top physicians. The campaign worked well and the combination started recording brisk sales.

But there was a problem. Fortwin had started exhibiting some serious side effects; patients would have difficulty in breathing or the blood pressure would shoot up. Chakroborty once received a dressing down from a top surgeon in Bangalore. As it was a copycat product, Ranbaxy obviously did not have access to all the information about the medicine. Back in Delhi, Chakroborty read up every bit of published information on Fortwin. Finally, he came across an article which said that Fortwin usage had to be individualized. The one millilitre pack was not mandatory for all. Doctors were advised to first inject one-fourth of the dosage and wait. The rest of the dosage was to be injected only if the patient's eyelids did not droop in the next two to three minutes. Chakroborty knew he had the answer. It was too good a marketing gimmick to let slip.

Chakroborty now came up with the 'Incremental Dosage' concept for Fortwin. New literature was published and a new campaign launched. Fortwin went on to become a top brand of the company. And Calmpose got a second lease of life.

4

The Push into Antibiotics

By the early-1970s, penicillin's glorious innings in the world pharmaceutical market was close to an end. In 1928, when bacteriologist Alexander Fleming discovered the germ-killing properties of the 'mould juice' secreted by *penicillium*, he knew he had hit upon something which had tremendous medical value. But Fleming could not make enough penicillin to be used in practice, and his discovery was dismissed as a mere laboratory experiment. A decade was to pass before a team of scientists at Oxford University rediscovered Fleming's work and revived research into the bacteria-killing mould. Although there was growing evidence of penicillin's effectiveness, the British, whose country was being bombarded as the Second World War raged, were unable to continue with the necessary research. The Oxford team turned to the United States for help. Inspired by the possibility of saving lives and of producing the world's first 'wonder drug', Pfizer offered its assistance.

In 1941, Pfizer was among the companies which responded to an appeal by the United States government to join a high-stakes race to see which company could develop a way to mass-produce the world's first 'wonder drug'. Beginning with fermentation experiments conducted with a team from Columbia University, Pfizer would, over the next three years, take enormous risks in devoting its energies to penicillin production. The substance was highly unstable, and initial yields were discouragingly low. Yet, Pfizer was determined to succeed in the quest to mass-produce this life-saving new drug.

As Pfizer's expertise increased, the company moved from surface fermentation in flasks to deep-tank fermentation. In the fall of 1942, Pfizer scientist Jasper Kane suggested a radically different approach, proposing that the company attempt to produce penicillin using the same deep-tank fermentation methods it had perfected for citric acid. This was tremendously risky because it would require Pfizer to curtail the production of citric acid and other well-established products, while it focussed on the development of penicillin. It could have placed the company's existing fermentation facilities in danger of becoming contaminated by the notoriously mobile *penicillium* spores.

Pfizer's senior management met in a small room in the company's Brooklyn (New York) plant to weigh the options and they took the leap. They voted to invest millions of dollars—putting their own assets as Pfizer stockholders at stake—to buy the equipment and facilities needed for deep-tank fermentation. Pfizer purchased a nearby vacant ice plant, and employees worked around the clock to convert it and perfect the complex production process. The plant was up and running in just four months, and soon Pfizer was producing five times more penicillin than originally anticipated. The race to mass produce penicillin was over. Pfizer had emerged victorious, but the real winners were the millions of people who were to benefit from the wonder drug. Penicillin was a turning point in human history—the first real defence against bacterial infection. By 1944, Pfizer had become the world's leading producer of penicillin.

Recognizing the superiority of the Pfizer process and desperate for massive quantities of penicillin to aid in the war effort, the United States government authorized nineteen companies to produce the antibiotic using Pfizer's deep-tank fermentation techniques, which the company had agreed to share with its competitors. However, despite their access to Pfizer's technology, none of these companies could come close to Pfizer's production levels and quality. Indeed, Pfizer produced 90 per cent of the penicillin that went ashore with the Allied forces at Normandy on D-Day in 1944 and more than half of all the penicillin used by the Allies for the rest of the war. It was, without a trace of doubt, the drug of the century.

*

Though Ranbaxy was making good profits on Calmpose, tranquillizers could never be a big business. The company was certain that the future lay in antibiotics. However, it did not know what drug to launch. By 1973, antibiotics like penicillin, tetracycline and streptomycin were at the end of their life cycle. As a result, Ranbaxy did not take up these drugs for development. Around this time, the company had formed a New Products Committee with the brief to identify new products for development. It was during one of the meetings of this committee in 1973 that K.G.S. 'Gopal' Nanda, a former medical adviser to Pfizer and now an adviser to Ranbaxy, emphatically announced that semi-synthetic penicillin was going to change the world of antibiotics. The drug he suggested for development was ampicillin.

Ranbaxy was no stranger to ampicillin, having imported the drug and introduced it as Roscillin along with Calmpose. Just like Roche had not bothered to get its diazepam patent registered in India, Beecham, which held the ampicillin patent, had ignored India while getting its patents registered.

But since Ranbaxy was importing ampicillin, it was three times as expensive as penicillin. It was no surprise, then, that the launch was a failure and Ranbaxy withdrew the drug from the market. Moreover, all ampicillin imports were canalized through the government-owned State Trading Corporation. This would have made any company's ampicillin business totally dependent on the government's whims and fancies. With the country perennially short of foreign exchange in those days, ampicillin imports could be axed without any notice.

*

Now, in 1973, with the possibility of in-house production of ampicillin opening up, Ranbaxy revived its ampicillin plans. The scientists working for the company told the management that they could bring down the price difference between penicillin and ampicillin by half. Gopinath and his men were told to develop a non-infringing process to produce ampicillin.

In 1974, Ranbaxy applied for a licence to produce ampicillin. Though the country's annual requirement for the drug was estimated at around three tonnes, Ranbaxy demanded a licence for five tonnes, anticipating a surge in demand in the near future. The bureaucrats were aghast. The country had just seen a wave of nationalization of banks and insurance companies—a move by Indira Gandhi's government to break the stranglehold of the private sector in the world of finance. The Ranbaxy request was ridiculous, considering that the government was out to break monopolies and set up the Monopolies & Restrictive Trade Practices Commission soon after.

Ranbaxy, however, remained firm on a five-tonne production. A high-level meeting of bureaucrats was called; it included the Cabinet Secretary, the country's topmost bureaucrat. Ranbaxy was represented at the meeting by

Bhai Mohan Singh, Dr Singh and Bimal Raizada. After much argument, the government agreed to give Ranbaxy a licence for five tonnes, provided it sold half the production to other companies making ampicillin formulations. Ranbaxy agreed to the condition. Since the State Trading Corporation was distributing bulk ampicillin in the country, Bhai Mohan Singh suggested that Ranbaxy be allowed to sell to it. The government did not object and Ranbaxy got the ampicillin licence in 1975. Devinder Singh Brar was to make this Ranbaxy's second major success story after Calmpose.

*

After acquiring a degree in engineering from the Thapar Institute of Technology in Patiala and a degree in business administration from the Faculty of Management Studies, Delhi University, Brar was working with the Associated Cement Companies (ACC), a Tata-controlled company at the time, which was the country's largest cement producer. Though his parents wanted him to become a civil servant, Brar was firmly opposed to the idea and, instead, chose a career in the corporate world. ACC had posted him in Mumbai but his parents were keen that he should come to Delhi since they had settled in Chandigarh after Brar's father, a bureaucrat, retired from service. However, Brar was not able to get a job to his liking in north India.

Brar's family also followed the Radhasoami Satsang of Beas. After his mother told the spiritual leader that she wanted Brar to find a job in the north, the Maharaj Ji mentioned this to Dr Singh. Never the one to say no to his spiritual guru, Dr Singh met Brar on his very next visit to Mumbai. At that time, there was nothing to suggest that the Indian pharmaceutical industry would one day become a sunrise industry with a global footprint. Hence, it was not even a blip on the radar screen of most young business executives. Still, Brar agreed to come on board once Dr Singh unveiled his vision to him.

Though Dr Singh's vision of making Ranbaxy a global player in the pharmaceutical business was yet to emerge, Brar realized that the man was extremely serious about his work and had already taken steps to pitch Ranbaxy as a player of reckoning in the domestic market. Ranbaxy's research and development centre was functional and it had achieved a success in the marketplace with its diazepam. It was one of the first Indian pharmaceutical companies to take up backward integration and set up a facility for bulk drugs. Brar knew that a pharmaceutical company's success in regulated markets depended on the control over its raw material. Any constraint on raw material availability could affect the company's brand strength and profitability. Ranbaxy, with the Calmpose success under its belt, had demonstrated that it understood the importance of such backward integration very well.

In 1977, Brar left the country's largest cement company in Mumbai and packed his bags for Delhi to join the still-obscure pharmaceutical company with a turnover of only Rs 6 crore. So far, Brar's only exposure to the company was the signboard on its Okhla factory seen from the train whenever he travelled to Mumbai.

Even at the time he joined Ranbaxy, Brar found it to be a family-oriented company with few professionals on its rolls. Decision-making powers remained with only a handful of people. Relatives of Bhai Mohan Singh working in the company were fiercely loyal to him. Still, he found a cohesive group of people working together. There was space for him and his ideas, however radically different they might be. There was scope to entertain controversies and people were encouraged to experiment with new ideas and change things in order to get better results. Though the company was small at that time, it had all the attributes of a modern and forward-thinking organization.

Though Dr Singh was focusing on the backward integration of Ranbaxy's operations, Bhai Mohan Singh was in favour of pushing exports in order to drive the company's profitability. The government had launched several export promotion schemes, one of which was to grant special import licences to exporters; the more a company exported the higher was its import quota. These licences soon became a passport to riches for many companies; with high tariff barriers on imports, huge profits were ensured as soon as a company was able to lay its hands on such a licence. Companies did not mind exporting at a loss, as these could be more than made up by profits in the domestic market through imports. Like many other Indian businessmen of his generation, Bhai Mohan Singh made the most of this opportunity by pushing exports to countries in Southeast Asia and Africa. What struck Brar was how Ranbaxy, in spite of its small size, was able to get these special import licences frequently.

Though Ranbaxy had set up its bulk drugs plant at Mohali to make diazepam and chlordiazepoxide, both tranquillizers, the unit was doing very badly. The technology was not up to the mark and the venture had totted up losses. Initially, it seemed that the backward integration was not a wise decision, as the expected benefits did not materialize. The 1975 directors' report noted that this 'was primarily because heavy imports of these bulk drugs did not allow the plant to operate at economic levels of production'. The funds raised from the 1973 public issue had been exhausted. One of the first things that Dr Singh asked Brar to do after he had joined was to review the product mix and turn around the plant.

At that time, Gopinath was making out a case for the production of analgin at Mohali on the grounds that it alone would best suit the configuration and size of the plant, even though Ranbaxy had the ampicillin licence under its belt. Ranbaxy was already selling analgin under the brand Ronalgin, using imported raw material. Gopinath had come very close to pushing his plans through. The technology for producing analgin was ready in-house and the company had already purchased the raw material required. It was a big investment for a small company.

After studying the proposal carefully, Brar came to the conclusion that the analgin project would only add to the company's losses. Instead, he suggested, the company should press on with its plans to produce ampicillin. A higher production of ampicillin, he argued, would help the company draw a larger quota of 6APA (6 amino-penicillic acid), the raw material for the drug, from the State Trading Corporation, which alone had the authority to import it.

All hell broke loose as soon as Brar had made his presentation. The attack was led by Gopinath, who could see his analgin plans going up in smoke. Others joined the chorus. Brar was denounced as a brash young executive fresh out of a business school, out to challenge conventional wisdom. But Brar stuck to his guns. More importantly, Dr Singh came out in his support. This helped. After a heated debate, the management committee cleared his proposal. Plans for analgin production were dropped and ampicillin production was on. Brar had announced his arrival. In 1977, Ranbaxy became the first company in the country to produce ampicillin. The very next year, Brar joined the executive committee of the company as a development manager.

*

Gopinath had proved his mettle first in 1973, when scientists from Regional Research Laboratory (RRL), Hyderabad, failed to upscale the diazepam technology at the Mohali plant. Bhai Mohan Singh and Dr Singh were livid. At this point, the company called in Gopinath and asked him to get the plant up and running, which he did in no time. The backward integration was successfully accomplished and Bhai Mohan Singh called Gopinath and his team to his office and gave cash rewards to all of them.

Even though Ranbaxy's research and development efforts were at a very nascent stage, Dr Singh was very demanding. He gave Gopinath a long list of drugs and demanded that he and his team come out with new process technologies for them. Gopinath never passed on the pressure from the top to his team. A good motivator of men, he would put in long hours of work with them, accompanying them to Mohali for testing out new technologies. In the evening he would send his driver to fetch beer, which he would chill himself. After a round of beer, he would take his team out to a fancy restaurant for dinner. And then they would be back in the factory working together.

Though fond of the good life, Gopinath was invariably badly dressed. He was in his mid-forties and had dark hair that fell to his shoulders. He would rarely untie his shoelaces, preferring to just slip on the shoes. At times he would come to work in torn trousers. He was a chain-smoker and later during his stay in Delhi developed a fondness for paan. Still, every member of his team was convinced that Gopinath was a great chemist. He had published many papers and was an articulate speaker. Whenever somebody went to him with a problem, Gopinath was never found wanting. His team comprised M. Sivakumaran (who had done his Ph.D under Gopinath's supervision at RRL, Jorhat, and was now his second-in-command), J.S. Sandhu, S.C. Srivastava, I.P.S. Grover (his father had joined Ranbaxy during the Lepetit years and became the production manager once the Italians left the company), Anil Sharma and Ashok Chaudhary.

When its ampicillin programme was at an advanced stage, it came to Ranbaxy's notice that somebody was putting up an ampicillin plant near Sonepat in Haryana with technology similar to the one developed by the Ranbaxy scientists. Further investigations by the company revealed that the plant belonged to one Dewan Pruthy—an importer of drugs. He was one of the country's leading distributors of vitamins and his customers included leading Indian pharmaceutical companies, one of them being Ranbaxy. As a result, he knew everybody at Ranbaxy.

The company believed that Gopinath was involved, going so far as to file a case in the Parliament street police station. Immediately afterwards, his services were terminated. The charges could never be proved in the courts, though the case dragged on for several years. When the other members of his team were grilled on why they had not reported the matter to the management, they all feigned ignorance, though rumours had been rife for six months before the scandal blew up. Gopinath's departure, however, was not to impact the rollout of Ranbaxy's very own ampicillin in 1977. The launch was followed soon after by a favourable change in the policy regime.

*

After amending the Patent Act in 1970, the government decided to come out with a new pharmaceutical policy in order to encourage domestic drug companies. A committee was formed under Jaisukhlal Hathi to prepare a blueprint for such a policy. The Hathi Committee suggested in 1975 that licences should be granted freely, all bulk drug producers should sell 30 per cent of the produce in the market in order to avoid monopolies and there should be parity between the formulations a company sold and the bulk drug it made. It fixed the ratio at 4:1 (four units of formulations for every unit of bulk drug made) for Indian companies and 2:1 for foreign companies. The Janata Party government led by Morarji Desai, which came to power in 1977, tweaked the ratio to 10:1 for Indian companies, while retaining the ratio of 2:1 for foreign companies. Clearly, the policy was heavily loaded in favour of Indian companies. Foreign companies, who did not want to invest in bulk drug capacities in India, got to sell lesser formulations.

At that time, the drug industry was rife with rumours

that the Hathi Committee report had been written in Bhai Mohan Singh's drawing room. As Ranbaxy had made investments in a bulk drug plant at Mohali, it could sell more formulations than other companies which did not have bulk drug operations. While it is true that Bhai Mohan Singh gave substantial inputs to the committee, just like, say, Yusuf Hamied of Cipla did, it is unlikely that the report was tailored to suit Ranbaxy's interests.

When Hathi was appointed chairman of the committee, Bhai Mohan Singh had every reason to feel elated; Hathi was close to S.K. Patil, a political heavyweight from the state of Maharashtra, who in turn was close to Bakshi Dalip Singh, Bhai Mohan Singh's father-in-law. Patil was a rising star within the Congress and Bhai Mohan Singh was too shrewd not to cultivate his friendship. In fact, it was Patil who had laid the foundation stone for Ranbaxy's Okhla factory on 27 May 1959. Patil, on his part, grew fond of Bhai Mohan Singh and started calling him his son-in-law.

When Patil became a minister in the Union cabinet, he would drop in frequently at Bhai Mohan Singh's house for a game of bridge. Though the two of them would be partners during the game, it was always Bhai Mohan Singh who paid the money after losing a game. Once, after a confrontation with Indira Gandhi on some issue, Patil had sent in his resignation. The first person he called for accommodation in case his resignation was accepted (which it was not) was Bhai Mohan Singh.

Hathi, who lived in Mumbai, was known to Patil and it was through his friend that Bhai Mohan Singh met Hathi. Soon, he called Hathi home for a drink. But Hathi did not want to be seen enjoying the hospitality of an industry person, lest he be accused of showing undue favours. He turned down Bhai Mohan Singh's invitation and similar requests. He finally agreed to come to Bhai Mohan Singh's house for dinner when his host assured him that a number of other CEOs of pharmaceutical companies would be present and everyone could talk informally.

This is not to say that Bhai Mohan Singh had no role to play in the committee's recommendations. He was the foremost representative of the pharmaceutical industry and made presentations on at least three occasions to the committee—first as the president of the All India Manufacturers' Organization, then as the chairman of the government's industrial advisory committee on drugs and pharmaceuticals, and finally as the chairman of the All India Drug Manufacturers' Association.

It was not just Ranbaxy which benefited from the Hathi Committee report. Several other companies did too. Along with the amended Patent Act, it would transform India into a leading bulk drug producer in the world. Several companies mushroomed, many of them in and around Hyderabad, supplying bulk drugs to leading pharmaceutical companies of the world. It would also make India the most complex pharmaceutical market in the world; success in India would be the ultimate test of a drug company's marketing skills.

*

When Chakroborty had moved from Chennai to Delhi as Ranbaxy's national sales manager in 1975, he found that the product literature was not of a very high standard and the training of the field force was virtually non-existent. His next few years were dedicated to improving the literature, packing as much scientific information as possible, and training the field force along the lines of what he had seen in the multinational companies he had worked for. Ranbaxy medical representatives were told to memorize the whole literature and taught the simple gesture of how to give a gift to a doctor ('Hold it with both your hands and give it with humility'), among other things. As a result, when Roscillin was re-launched in 1977, Ranbaxy's new-look field force was ready with better product literature.

Thanks to Chakroborty's efforts and Ranbaxy's first mover advantage, Roscillin became an instant success. It did particularly well in the South, where it became a household name, despite competition from Smith Kline & French. It went on to become not only one of the top five pharmaceutical brands in the country, but also one of the top two brands in the rural markets, the other being Crocin of Reckitt & Coleman (which later became Reckitt Benckiser after its global merger with Benckiser). The brand was gaining in volumes and the profitability was high; a third of the company's turnover and profits came from Roscillin in the early-1980s.

While the landed cost of the ampicillin imported by the State Trading Corporation was as high as Rs 2,100 per kg, Ranbaxy's cost of production came to only Rs 1,475 per kg. As any retail price for ampicillin fixed by the government had to be benchmarked against the import price, Ranbaxy made a tidy profit. Ranbaxy subsequently raised its ampicillin capacity from five tonnes to twenty-four tonnes and finally to 100 tonnes in 1984. When the patent on the drug expired in countries like Thailand and Malaysia in 1982, Ranbaxy started exporting it to these countries.

Thanks to Roscillin, Ranbaxy's investments in bulk drug manufacturing had started paying off by 1979. 'The move has put Ranbaxy ahead of other pharmaceutical companies,' the 1979 annual report exulted. It pointed out that Ranbaxy had gone ahead with bulk drug manufacturing at a time when other companies were hesitating to get into this capital-intensive activity with a long gestation period, in view of the strict control on prices and profitability. Ranbaxy, it said, began work even before the government's drug policy made it statutory for pharmaceutical companies to manufacture bulk drugs. Besides, against the formulations to bulk drug ratio fixed at 10:1, at Ranbaxy the ratio was as high as 3:1.

So heady was the mood inside the company with the success of ampicillin that in 1982, when other companies had started drawing up plans for launching amoxycillin, a next-generation anti-infective, Ranbaxy just ignored the opportunity. There was an internal debate in the company on the issue. However, the marketing team felt that amoxycillin and ampicillin were competing products and amoxycillin would eat into Roscillin sales. The company decided to give it a miss.

It was an erroneous decision and proved to be the costliest miss ever for Ranbaxy. Amoxycillin far outlived ampicillin as an anti-infective. Twenty years later, while ampicillin had been all but wiped out from the sales counters, amoxycillin was still going strong. Ranbaxy was able to set the mistake right only in the mid-1990s, by which time amoxycillin, and not ampicillin, was the favoured prescription of doctors.

Once it had realized its mistake, Ranbaxy knew that the only way it could enter the amoxycillin market was by buying out a leading brand. It had been eyeing a Mumbai-based company called Gufic Biosciences since the early 1990s. Though a late entrant in the amoxycillin business (Cipla had taken the first mover's advantage with its Novanox), by the late 1980s, Gufic's brand, Mox, had emerged as the undisputed leader in the marketplace within five years of its launch. By 1994, Ranbaxy knew that it had to acquire Mox if it was to survive in the amoxycillin market.

Since Ranbaxy had no experience in mergers and acquisitions, it appointed Uday Kotak, an upcoming Gujarati investment banker running a company called Kotak Mahindra, to handle the deal. Dr Singh, Brar and Vijay Kaul, finance director, flew to Mumbai to meet Kotak. Soon, Kotak set up a meeting with Jayesh P. Choksi, the owner of Gufic. Though initially reluctant to part with his brand, he finally came around and sold all his brands, including Mox, to Ranbaxy in 1995 for around Rs 45 crore. The mistake of the early-1980s had been corrected and Ranbaxy found itself at the top of the amoxycillin market.

*

Even when it had launched Roscillin, Ranbaxy was aware that the technology for the production of ampicillin was simple. There were a large number of producers in Italy, the bulk-drug capital of Europe, who were willing to share the technology with anybody who was willing to pay. The fears proved to be correct; in a span of a few short years, a large number of small ampicillin producers had mushroomed all over the country. If Ranbaxy had to sustain the momentum provided by Roscillin, it had to launch other anti-infective drugs faster than its competitors.

In 1977, Ranbaxy added two more antibiotics to its portfolio: doxycycline under the brand Tetradox and rifampicin under the brand Tibirim. Ranbaxy was also the first in the country to start the production of doxycycline after a hard-fought corporate battle. The government had decided to issue two licences for the production of the drug. While it had decided to hand over one to IDPL, Ranbaxy and a company called Euphoric Drugs were in the race for the other. Euphoric Drugs told the government that it would import the technology from Pfizer in the United States. Ranbaxy, by contrast, had registered a patent for a new process to develop the drug. Finally, Ranbaxy won the battle on the grounds of protection to domestic research and development. Doxycycline, however, failed to live up to the expectations and never became a blockbuster product.

In late-1979, Ranbaxy introduced Sporidex and Sporidine, brands which belonged to the cephalosporin group of new antibiotics which had grabbed the attention of the medical profession the world over. These were also derived from penicillin and had a wider spectrum of application than ampicillin. Sporidex too turned out to be a big success; it ranked amongst the top ten pharmaceutical brands of the country soon after launch, even though it was pitted against Glaxo's Phexin.

After ampicillin and cephalosporins, Ranbaxy was to consolidate its hold on the anti-infective market with its ciprofloxacin formulation sold under the brand Cifran. The person responsible for this was O.P. Sood.

*

After working in various hospitals in India and abroad, O.P. Sood had joined Vadodara-based Squibb Sarabhai in 1972 as associate medical director of research. Twelve years later he joined Ranbaxy. The shift defied logic. At that time, Sarabhai was the country's leading pharmaceutical group and Ranbaxy was still far behind. Sood had done well for himself, having risen to become the medical director of Surat Geigy, a joint venture of the Sarabhai group and Geigy (the company became SG Pharmaceuticals after Ciba merged with Geigy). But the signs that the empire was sinking because of infighting within the Sarabhai family were already evident.

Sood wanted to return from Gujarat to his hometown of Delhi. Though there was nothing in Ranbaxy at that time to attract a prospective employee, he still decided to join the company as the chief of medical and professional services. Apart from functions like training of medical representatives and liaisoning with the medical fraternity and the government, Sood was also responsible for the identification of new products for development and was instrumental in setting up the New Products Committee. His brief was to pick out those products for development in India, which could be good revenue earners over a long period of time.

Ranbaxy was desperately in need of another big seller like Calmpose. Roscillin, which had held the company in good stead in the late-1970s and early-1980s, was running out of steam as certain bacteria had developed a resistance to it. The New Products Committee zeroed in on fluoroquinolones. Not only were fluoroquinolones active against a wider spectrum of bacteria as compared to semi-synthetic penicillin like ampicillin and cephalosporins, they were also active against bacteria which had developed a resistance to ampicillin. Besides, unlike semi-synthetic penicillin or cephalosporins, fluoroquinolones did not have to be put through a fermentation process as these drugs are fully synthetic. As a result, the cost of producing fluoroquinolones was cheaper.

But Sood's proposal met with stiff resistance from within Ranbaxy, especially from the marketing department, which again felt that fluoroquinolones would eat into the sales of Roscillin. But Sood received support from Brar in the New Products Committee. Finally, it was decided that the company would produce all the three fluoroquinolones: ciprofloxacin, ofloxacin and norfloxacin. While Bayer held the patents on ciprofloxacin, Hoechst held the patents for ofloxacin and Merck for norfloxacin.

Soon, Ranbaxy's research and development department had developed these fluoroquinolones using non-infringing processes. It was decided to put these brands under Stancare, the new marketing division set up within the company for new products. Ciprofloxacin was launched as Cifran, ofloxacin as Zanocin and norfloxacin as Norbectin.

*

Cifran was launched on 16 May 1989, Brar's wedding anniversary. Chakroborty, who by now had four doctors with MD degrees working for him in the marketing department, came out with a dramatic campaign for the drug. So far, all pharmaceutical companies would talk of minimum inhibitory concentration as an index of the efficacy of any anti-bacterial. It measured the extent to which the spread of bacteria in the body had been contained. Chakroborty knew that if he had to break new ground, this concept had to be blown to pieces. By now, Pfizer had introduced the concept of minimum bacterial concentration. Chakroborty quickly latched on to it. Instead of detailing the containment of the bacteria, the campaign would talk of how the bacteria had been killed. Cifran was positioned as a drug that could kill bacteria at low concentration. When the campaign was unveiled to doctors, the response was tremendous. Chakroborty knew he had a winner on his hands. 'In pharmaceuticals, marketing is all about making a story out of a product,' Chakroborty who retired in the mid-1990s and settled down in Salt Lake, Kolkata, would remember later.

Confident that it had a success in its hands, the company planned a big launch. It had embarked on a huge pre-launch publicity campaign with the doctors and spent time and money on training the field staff. The excitement levels were high. Ranbaxy had just lost the war to Cipla over ofloxacin. Cipla had launched its ofloxacin before Ranbaxy and the latter could make little headway in sales. Ranbaxy did not want a repeat of that in the case of ciprofloxacin. So it had left no stone unturned in preparing the ground for Cifran's launch.

As the launch date neared, and the stocks were packed and ready for shipment, one executive stumbled upon the fact, to the company's horror, that there was another Cifran in the marketplace. The company had to settle this trademark issue before the launch or else it would have been forced to call it off. For a moment, it seemed that all the money and energy spent on preparing the launch was in vain. R.K. Arora, the general manager (sales), broke down. A change in brand and packaging would take at least another couple of months. On the other hand, rival firms were working overtime to launch their ciprofloxacin. Brar had to act fast and decisively.

Detailed inquiries revealed that the brand belonged to a company in Mumbai running a dairy business. This company's owners were not even aware that their trademark was under a threat of violation from Ranbaxy. Ranbaxy had to fork out a little over Rs 3 lakh to buy out the brand.

The deal was sealed a day before the launch.

This was not the only problem facing Brar and Chakroborty. They came to know a few days before the launch that Ahmedabad-based Cadila Pharmaceuticals, a company promoted by teacher-turned-entrepreneur Ramanbhai Patel in 1952, was planning to import ciprofloxacin and introduce it in the market. An analysis of the landed cost suggested that Cadila would have to sell at a price of Rs 25 a tablet in order to make decent profits, a fact which investigations confirmed. Ranbaxy decided to give a nasty shock to Cadila by pricing Cifran at Rs 18 a tablet. The trick worked and Cadila was left gasping.

Cifran proved to be another runaway success. 'Cifran is setting new standards of therapeutic efficacy in the treatment of infections and has emerged as the anti-bacterial of choice,' Ranbaxy's 1989-90 directors' report said. Cifran became the first Indian brand to cross a turnover of Rs 10 crore within the first year of its launch. Ranbaxy even acquired a company, Hyderabad-based Vorin Laboratories, for the bulk production of ciprofloxacin but subsequently divested its stake in it in a management buyout.

*

What made Cifran's success sweeter was that around the same time, Ranbaxy came out with its first blockbuster over-the-counter product. Ranbaxy first got into over-the-counter business in November 1977, when it had launched Garlic Pearls. In 1979, it added the Naturelle range of shampoos to the business. However, by 1983, it was clear to the company that these products were not its core strengths and the business was discontinued.

In 1989, Ranbaxy re-entered the segment and launched Revital. The request for the product had actually come from V.N. Bhalla, the managing director of Ranbaxy Malaysia. He had observed that ginseng-based products were selling well in the market and was pestering Brar for a similar product. Brar had seen a similar product in Switzerland packed in soft gelatine capsules. He acceded to Bhalla's request and the product was developed and shipped to Malaysia. But the product just did not move in the market, in contrast to Bhalla's projections.

One day, Brar was sitting with an acquaintance who also happened to be a 'clairvoyant'. Brar told him about Revital's indifferent sales and how disappointed they were by it. The 'clairvoyant' immediately told Brar that Revital would be a huge success in India. Brar heeded his advice and started making preparations for the launch of Revital in the Indian market. Ranbaxy had launched a similar product in the past, a multi-vitamin called Ranvit, but it had flopped miserably. Meanwhile, Glaxo's competing brand, Becosules, was growing from strength to strength.

While travelling with Brar in his car one day, Chakroborty told him that he did not want to market Revital on the basis of its scientific properties but pitch it using a more sublime concept. If Brar agreed, Chakroborty said that he would work on the concept at home and, therefore, begged not to be disturbed. At home, Chakroborty started taking Revital, one tablet every day. Soon, he could feel a change. There was a newfound energy running through his body. The tonic properties ginseng is credited with seemed to be having their effect. He could experience it, yet he could not explain what it was. As he was mulling over this problem, he hit upon the Revital punchline: 'Better experienced than explained'. Revital sales too crossed Rs 10 crore within a year of its launch in January 1989.

A few days after the launch, a small Delhi company approached Ranbaxy and said that it already owned the Revital brand name and that Ranbaxy would have to either withdraw its brand or pay an amount between Rs 1.5 crore and Rs 2 crore as compensation. The company was able to prove to the Ranbaxy lawyers that its Revital did have genuine sales of Rs 6.5 lakh. After bargaining, Ranbaxy paid the company Rs 15 lakh to buy out its brand. This initial hiccup over, Revital sales were brisk from day one.

*

With Cifran, Zanocin, Sporidex and Roscillin, Ranbaxy now had four anti-infectives in its kitty, each of which was recording brisk sales. Chakroborty's job now was to position the four in such way that one did not eat into the sales of the other.

Roscillin was slipping down the value chain and it was the lowest-priced of the four. It was most popular in the rural markets. Sporidex, which was priced at double the rate of Roscillin, came next and was targeted at urban consumers. Then there was Cifran, which was prescribed for urinary tract and chest infections. Right on top was Zanocin, positioned as the most powerful anti-bacterial and carrying a price tag of Rs 28 to Rs 30 per tablet. It was targeted at the most successful doctors, keeping in mind its profile.

Ranbaxy had become the country's top anti-infective drug company and Chakroborty had earned a reputation as the foremost pharmaceutical marketing brain in the country.

When Ranbaxy had embarked on its anti-infective journey, it was not even amongst the top twenty-five pharmaceutical companies in the country. By 1981, it was placed among the top five Indian pharmaceutical companies of the day. By the end of 1982, Ranbaxy ranked fourth among domestic pharmaceutical companies and twelfth among all pharmaceutical companies, Indian as well as multinational, operating in India. By 1989-90, it had emerged as the largest earner of foreign exchange in the drugs and pharmaceutical sector, exporting over half its production of bulk drugs. By 1990-91, Ranbaxy had climbed to the second spot amongst Indian pharmaceutical companies.

Ranbaxy became India's largest pharmaceutical company in 1993-94, apart from being the number one exporter and the largest producer of pharmaceutical substances, accounting for almost 15 per cent of the national output. And the man who put up these production capacities for Ranbaxy was Pushpinder Bindra.

*

Born and brought up in Dehradun, Bindra secured a degree in engineering from the Punjab Engineering College in Chandigarh before acquiring an MBA from the University of Detroit in the US. In 1978, Bindra was back in India, having signed up with fast-moving consumer goods major Procter & Gamble (then known as Richardson Hindustan) in Mumbai. The company's flagship brand was Vicks—the ultimate treatment for cough and cold. It also marketed the Merrill range of prescription drugs. But in the late 1970s, the Cincinnati-based Richardson Merrill Inc. sold that business to Dow Chemicals. Richardson Hindustan's parent thus became Richardson Vicks Inc.

It is the dream of every young business-school graduate to cut his teeth in a large multinational company. Bindra could not have asked for a better start to his career. However, within a couple of years, he was a disillusioned man. Because of the patent laws, the multinationals were not getting new drugs and technology into the country. They were flogging old technology in India; the machines imported were usually picked up from scrapyards abroad. There were no signs of investments in bulk drug manufacturing. All told, Bindra felt that the prospects for someone seeking a career in manufacturing were limited.

In 1980, at a time when nobody would want to work for an Indian pharmaceutical company, Bindra started talking to Ranbaxy and a year later, he was on the company's rolls. Though Bindra had been warned by his friends and relatives, nothing had prepared him for the culture shock that awaited him when he took up office at Okhla as the production planning and inventory control manager. Unlike Procter & Gamble, where everybody spoke in English, people either spoke in Punjabi or Hindi at Ranbaxy. He was also shocked at the sight of male secretaries taking down dictation and typing letters.

By the early 1980s, Ranbaxy was running out of formulations capacity, thanks largely to the roaring success of Roscillin. It now needed additional production capacity. The safest option for the company would have been to expand at Mohali. Yet, it chose to locate the new capacity at Dewas, in Madhya Pradesh. There were several reasons for choosing this location. One, since Dewas is located in a backward area, Ranbaxy would get some tax benefits. Two, the company was making substantial imports by then and Dewas was closer to the Mumbai port than Mohali was. Three, it would cut the costs involved in reaching Ranbaxy products to the southern and western markets of the country.

The plant was put on the drawing board in 1982, and it was completed and commissioned in record time by December 1983. Dr Singh had set the deadline and pushed Bindra and his team to meet it. Ranbaxy was never able to complete a greenfield project with such speed again.

In 1989, Ranbaxy made an investment in another production unit, this time a bulk drugs plant at Taonsa in Punjab. The place where the plant came up was called Bhai Mohan Singh Nagar. This plant started with the production of doxycycline, cephalexin, ranitidine and ampicillin. The decision to locate the plant at Taonsa was prompted by the fact that it was only around 40 km from Mohali, where all those with an expertise in chemistry were based. Ranbaxy also got some tax incentives for investing in Taonsa.

In 1991, Ranbaxy added a bulk drugs facility at Dewas. Though the place was affected by acute water shortage, the company went ahead with the investment. Punjab was torn by militancy and this had cast a shadow on the state's future. Though Ranbaxy had not lost even a single day's production because of terrorist threats, it thought it prudent to make investments outside the state.

In 1993-94, the company put up a fermentation plant at Paonta Sahib, in Himachal Pradesh, where it again got some tax benefits for investing in a backward area. In 1995, the company added a formulations plant there, investing Rs 50 crore. Ranbaxy acquired two more facilities—one in Pune and the other in Goa—when it acquired Mumbai-based Croslands in 1995.

As Ranbaxy's global business grew, not only was Bindra required to churn out larger volumes, he was also expected to produce more drugs. 'The name of the game one day is going to be producing maybe just a single tablet of a drug for some customer. Ranbaxy is headed for that level of specialization,' Bindra said at his spacious Mohali office.

With more investments coming in, Bindra started importing the best equipment from all over the world by the late 1990s. While the earlier equipment was either the product of reverse engineering or procured from the lowest cost supplier, Ranbaxy was now sourcing only the best.

In all the units, steps were taken from the beginning to ensure that the final product was always of the best quality. In the early 1980s, the company exported several drugs in dosage forms to various countries in Asia and Africa. Once there were complaints about unappealing packaging from Malaysia. Bindra was summoned by Dr Singh and shown samples from the consignment. The packaging looked perfect to Bindra. Annoyed with Dr Singh for pulling him up, Bindra went to a chemist shop in the evening, picked up all multinational products from there and showed it to his boss the next morning. Bindra wanted to silence Dr Singh by showing him that his packaging was at par with that of foreign companies. But Dr Singh was not impressed. 'This is not my benchmark,' he told Bindra, flinging the packaging back at him. It immediately struck Bindra that Dr Singh was not competing against Indian subsidiaries of multinationals; he was thinking of taking on the parent companies of these subsidiaries.

A sound manufacturing base finally became a critical component of Ranbaxy's global strategy. All its world markets would be fed out of its cost-effective production facilities in India. The advantages were much the same as in other industries. The low cost of labour enabled Indian companies to produce goods and services at a fraction of the cost compared to their counterparts in the developed world where wages were high. The market for generic medicines in the world was always extremely price-sensitive. Drug companies in the West would often turn to low cost suppliers like Ranbaxy for generic products.

5

The Cracks in the Family

In 1989, Bhai Mohan Singh split the family business between his three sons—Dr Singh, Bhai Manjit Singh and Analjit Singh. The business had grown and each of them wanted their own space. Corporate India had just seen two very unpleasant family splits: one in the Birla family and the other in the Modi family. The nasty infighting had leaked to the media, which fed salacious details to readers. Bhai Mohan Singh wanted to avoid a similar situation. Till then, there were no family fissures that were visible to outsiders. Besides, few in his family had survived beyond sixty-five years and he wanted to divide the family assets amicably during his lifetime.

Thus, Dr Singh got control of Ranbaxy, Manjit of Montari Industries and Analjit of Max India. In addition, Manjit got the family properties at the posh Golf Links and Prithviraj Road in New Delhi and Analjit got Ranbaxy's Okhla factory. The Aurangzeb Road property had been divided into four parts—one part for Bhai Mohan Singh and one each for the three sons. Since Ranbaxy was the largest

Family photo on the occasion of Bhai Mohan Singh being awarded the Padma Shri for his public services. *From left*: Dr Singh, Maheep (Bhai Manjit Singh's wife), Avtar Mohan Singh, Analjit, Nirmaljit (Dr Singh's wife) and Bhai Mohan Singh.

company of the lot, Manjit and Analjit also received cash compensation of around Rs 1 crore each.

Bhai Mohan Singh had brought up his family in a traditional way. The drawing room of his house had impressions in henna of six pairs of hands—that of each son and his wife. The impression is put soon after marriage as a mark of solidarity with the family and respect to the parents. What people did not know was that things had changed. In the end, there was much rancour within the family and the split was so bitter that the corporate world had not seen any like it. Each of the three brothers had embarked on a different destiny.

*

Manjit was born in January 1947, four years after Dr Singh and three months before the family moved from Rawalpindi to New Delhi. He had a happy childhood, divided between school at St. Columba's, swimming and playing lawn tennis at the Delhi Gymkhana and bicycle rides to Khan Market to buy books. During summer every year, the family would go to Kashmir for four weeks. In 1958, Manjit was sent to Doon School, where Dr Singh was already studying. Amongst Manjit's classmates were future stars of Indian politics like Sanjay Gandhi, Kamal Nath, Naveen Patnaik and Akbar 'Dumpy' Ahmad.

After clearing his Senior Cambridge examinations in 1964, Manjit returned to Delhi to study in St. Stephen's College and completed his graduation in 1968. While his father wanted him to enrol in a business school abroad, he himself had other plans. He had fallen in love with Maheep, an acquaintance, and wanted to marry her. His plans would go awry if he went abroad. So he decided to stay on in Delhi and enrolled in law college.

But destiny had something else in store for him. The Lepetit crisis happened and Manjit ended up joining Ranbaxy in 1968 as a management trainee on a monthly stipend of Rs 1,500 (he was allowed to have lunch with his father at work). Over the next twenty-odd years, he went on to handle several functions ranging from purchase, exports and imports, and overseeing the consumer products division which included products like Naturelle shampoo, Garlic Pearls and vitamin tablets for children.

Manjit was inducted into Ranbaxy's board of directors in 1977 along with his elder brother. But Dr Singh rose through the hierarchy faster: in April 1982, he was promoted as managing director of the company for a period of five years and, in April 1987, he was made the vice-chairman and managing director for five years. All this while, Manjit continued as the commercial director.

Manjit, by his own admission, had differences with

Dr Singh right from his first day at work. While Dr Singh was focussed on pharmaceuticals, Manjit wanted to diversify into other areas and began scouting for opportunities. As far back as the early 1970s, he had developed a passion for setting up a hotel in the heart of Delhi. In 1972, Ranbaxy bought shares in a company called Tara Hotels, which then became its subsidiary. The 1972 directors' report to the shareholders of Tara Hotel noted that the company was negotiating with a foreign party for collaboration, and it was hoped that the company would be able to take up the project that year itself.

By now, the family had moved from the Prithviraj Road residence to the complex of four houses on Aurangzeb Road. All the four houses were interconnected, so that everyone could have the comfort of being with the family along with the required privacy. The construction laws at that time said that at least two acres of land was required for a hotel. The Aurangzeb Road plot had 2.7 acres between the four houses. Manjit suggested that a hotel could be constructed on the site in a joint venture with a global hospitality major. The land would be the family's equity contribution. Everybody agreed and the land was parked in a new company called Delhi Guest Houses Ltd in which Bhai Mohan Singh and his three sons were equal shareholders.

After negotiating with a host of global hotel chains, Manjit tied up with Hong Kong-based Regent International, a new and upcoming chain of luxury hotels. The architecture of the hotel, along with the design of the rooms and the layout of the restaurants, was finalized and submitted for the local administration's approval. While most of the other approvals did not take much time to come through, the Delhi Urban Arts Commission objected to the plan on the grounds that it did not conform to the Master Plan for Lutyens's Delhi (the zone falling in the area designed by the architect of New Delhi, Edward Lutyens). The hotel was to have eight floors and it was argued that the top floor would overlook the Mahatma Gandhi memorial on Tees January Marg located nearby.

Manjit made numerous representations to successive governments, but in vain. This was one of the rare instances where Bhai Mohan Singh's awesome political connections did not work.

Then, in 1980, Manjit convinced his school friend, Sanjay Gandhi, that the proposed hotel conformed to the Master Plan in all respects. Sanjay Gandhi promised to help. Finally, there seemed to be light at the end of the tunnel for Manjit and the dream he had pursued for over a decade. But Sanjay Gandhi died in an air crash soon after and Manjit was back to square one. Meanwhile, there were murmurs within the family that, in the light of all this, the hotel was not a very good business proposal. The project was given a burial.

Delhi Guest Houses continued to exist and own the four properties. Ranbaxy held shares of the company till 2001 when the stock was taken over by a private company owned by Malvinder Singh and Shivinder Singh, Dr Singh's sons.

Almost twenty years after the project was abandoned, Manjit continued to maintain that corporate rivalry did it in. A hotel on Aurangzeb Road would have cut into the business of two hotels in the vicinity—Claridges Hotel, which was right opposite Bhai Mohan Singh's house, and Taj Mahal Hotel run by the Tata-owned Indian Hotels. But more than the corporate rivals, Manjit blamed his elder brother for not supporting the project sufficiently because he did not want to diversify into areas unrelated to pharmaceuticals.

After the jinxed hotel venture, Manjit again started looking around for opportunities. He examined various business options ranging from sponge iron to two-wheeler tyres, leather and pharmaceutical intermediates. He finally zeroed in on pharmaceutical ingredients. A few products were shortlisted and the technology to produce them identified. But the business plan turned out to be too expensive for Manjit and this plan too had to be scrapped.

The only option left for Manjit was chemicals and he, therefore, opted for pesticides. The family invested in a new company called Montari Chemicals (Mon from Bhai Mohan Singh and Tari from Avtar Kaur's nickname), which put up a plant for basic chemicals inside the sprawling Ranbaxy complex at Bhai Mohan Singh Nagar in Punjab. A Chandigarh-based formulations company, Kisan Chemicals, was also taken over for this purpose. Its plant was subsequently shifted to Bhai Mohan Singh Nagar and the company was merged into Montari Chemicals to form Montari Industries. On 1 October 1988, Manjit was appointed the managing director of Montari Industries, as a part of the family settlement. As a result, he resigned from the post of commercial director at Ranbaxy and became a non-executive director. Things were going well for Manjit.

In 1988, Naina Lal, granddaughter of legendary industrialist Lala Karam Chand Thapar and at that time an investment banker with ANZ Grindlays (now with HSBC), approached Ranbaxy with a proposal. Bausch & Lomb, the United States-based eyewear major which owned the famous Ray-Ban brand of sunglasses, was keen on starting a venture in India to make contact lenses. Would Ranbaxy be interested? Bausch & Lomb was interested in the eye-care liquids market more than Ray-Ban sunglasses. It wanted to sell its products through chemists and not opticians. That is why it was on the lookout for an alliance with a company like Ranbaxy.

Bhai Mohan Singh accepted the offer and talks between the two parties began. As Dr Singh did not show much interest, Manjit expressed his interest in becoming a partner in the venture. Bhai Mohan Singh told Bausch & Lomb that Montari, and not Ranbaxy, would be their partner. Bausch & Lomb had no choice but to agree. The talks had progressed too far ahead to pull back now and start fresh negotiations with another party. Besides, Bhai Mohan Singh gave the assurance that Montari was a part of the same group and the venture could count on Ranbaxy's full support. Ranbaxy was indeed involved in giving shape to the joint venture. As the family separation was under way at that time, the agreement with Bausch & Lomb was signed by one of the investment companies that were to go to Bhai Manjit Singh. Bhai Mohan Singh roped in key Ranbaxy officials like Vinay Kaul to work out the details.

Soon, Manjit was on his way to Rochester to meet the Bausch & Lomb brass. The proposal he made at Rochester was nothing short of outrageous. As production of foreign brands like Ray-Ban was not allowed in India at that time, he said that the brand could be launched in the Indian market using either a prefix or a suffix! (Pepsi, for instance, was launched as Lehar Pepsi.) Surprisingly, Bausch & Lomb agreed. Meanwhile, back in India, hectic lobbying had started bearing fruit, and the government agreed to amend the rules on local manufacturing of foreign brands. Ray-Ban was to become the first foreign eyewear brand to be launched in India. Both Montari Industries and Bausch & Lomb took 40 per cent each in the joint venture, Bausch & Lomb India Pvt. Ltd, while 20 per cent equity was placed with the public.

This was perhaps the high-water mark of Manjit's career. Though his pet hotel never saw the light of the day, the pesticides business was off the block and he had brought one of the biggest brands in the world to India. A footwear export business was also on the anvil. Prompted by export incentives, Manjit set up Montari Leather in the late 1980s in technical collaboration with Bally of Switzerland for manufacturing footwear. The British Shoe Company of the United Kingdom had agreed to pick up the products for marketing in Europe. Again, Montari Industries was chosen to invest in the equity capital of Montari Leather.

As per the shareholders' agreement of Bausch & Lomb India, while Manjit became the managing director of the company, the president was to be jointly appointed by the two partners, the chief financial officer (CFO) would be a Bausch & Lomb nominee, while Montari Industries would provide secretarial services. By appointing his own man as the company secretary, Manjit could keep tabs on who was selling and buying into the company, a common practice amongst Indian businessmen. Both the partners had equal representation on the board of directors.

The good-natured and affable Manjit was able to attract people from multinational corporations and top Indian companies to work for Bausch & Lomb India. He liked to talk of his business as the Montari Group, of which Bausch & Lomb India was the crown jewel. Manjit knew that Bausch & Lomb India was different from his other two home-grown companies. In fact, he admired Bausch & Lomb's culture and had struck a good rapport with the company's top brass. He was particularly close to Bausch & Lomb's head in Europe, India-born Alex Kumar. As a result, he never tried to impose the Montari culture on this company and gave its president, Jaspal Bajwa, a free hand to run the company. Senior Bausch & Lomb India executives would say that Manjit shielded them from interference by the Montari management. On the contrary, for important meetings with bankers, he would take senior executives from the company along in order to showcase the managerial talent in his group.

But the honeymoon proved short-lived. Within the first year itself, it became evident that the company's breakeven projections were too ambitious. As its equity base was capitalized at just Rs 10 crore, the company ran short of money in the first year itself and had to go for a rights issue to stay afloat. Losses started mounting by the day as the company invested heavily in developing the market for its sunglasses. Soon it was time for more money to be pumped into the company. While Bausch & Lomb was prepared to infuse more money, Manjit found his hands tied. Montari Industries had started making losses and Montari Leather was headed in the same direction. The implication was clear: if the company was to become financially strong, he would have to reduce his stake. That would have meant the end of Manjit's dreams. Thus all Bausch & Lomb proposals for a rights issue got delayed.

Meanwhile, there was no improvement in the company's fortunes. By 1996, its net worth had eroded by 50 per cent and it faced the prospect of reporting to the Board for Industrial & Financial Reconstruction (BIFR) as required by the law. This would have affected Bausch & Lomb's image in the country and dampened the morale of its marketing team. The company however managed to ward off the crisis and get a reprieve of fifteen to eighteen months. While the losses would be arrested within this time, Bajwa and his men were hopeful that the two promoters would come to an understanding and money would get injected into the company.

But relationship between the two partners was deteriorating fast. To further complicate matters, Bausch & Lomb India terminated its contract with a Manjit-owned company called Vimoni (named after his children Vikramjit, Mohanjit and Niyamat) for the supply of bottles and grinding of lenses on the grounds that it was no longer viable. The upshot was that when Manjit's five-year term as managing director came to an end in 1997, it was not extended.

With the disagreements persisting, Manjit finally agreed to sell out of the company. All his nominees on the board gave undated resignation letters.

As news of Manjit's sell-out leaked to the media, the price of Bausch & Lomb India shares skyrocketed. Manjit had pledged almost his entire stock to raise funds. So with rising prices, the creditors sold the shares in the market, recovering their investments and returning the remainder to Manjit. Thus, even after buying him out of the joint venture in 1998, Bausch & Lomb's stake in the company went up only marginally from 40 per cent to 43 per cent.

To make investments in Bausch & Lomb, pesticides and leather, Montari Industries had decided to go for a rights issue of Rs 43 crore in March 1991. The stock markets were booming and it was decided to price the rights issue at Rs 35 per share as against the stock market price of Rs 70 per share. Unfortunately for Manjit, two days after the rights issue opened for a month, the markets crashed and the Montari Industries share price plummeted. The issue was grossly undersubscribed and against a target of Rs 43 crore, the company could muster only Rs 25 crore.

This put Manjit in a spot. Bausch & Lomb had already sent its share of money for the rights issue three months earlier and the money was lying in the bank. Other investments too had been committed and there was no way he could have backed out. Manjit decided to make up the deficit by raising debt from the market. Montari Industries borrowed almost Rs 25 crore through inter-corporate deposits at interest rates of up to 25 per cent per annum. The financial burden proved too much for the company and it soon became a sick company. Montari Leather too met with the same fate.

Manjit became a bitter man, blaming the family settlement for his ills.

*

Dr Singh and Manjit had very little in common. While his elder brother was serious and cold to all except his close friends and relatives, Manjit was fun-loving and fond of the good life. He loved to entertain and throw expensive parties. Dr Singh, on the other hand, would use very little of his entertainment allowance, as Raizada discovered while managing the finances at Ranbaxy. Two months before his death in July 1999, Dr Singh wanted to take one final vacation in Italy with his family. He called up his close friend Vivek Bharat Ram to make arrangements for his stay. Vivek, who had a joint venture with Italian clothing major Benetton, agreed but protested that Dr Singh's budget was too frugal for a decent hotel. Reminding him that it was a private holiday, Dr Singh raised the budget by $50 a day. This, at a time when he was one of the richest men in the country!

In many ways, Dr Singh was similar to his youngest brother, Analjit. Both were visionaries with a modern worldview and were capable of thinking ahead of their times. In addition, both of them were deeply spiritual; while Dr Singh was a follower of the Radhasoami Satsang, Analjit became a lifelong devotee of the Chinmaya Mission. Yet, the two also drifted apart.

*

Analjit was born in January 1954. He was deeply attached to his parents and his brothers in his formative years and the attachment grew as the years passed. There was a gap of eleven years between Analjit and Dr Singh. So, while he always looked up to him, he was also a little scared of him. On his part, Dr Singh was very fond of his youngest brother; he and his friends would call him 'Monkey' instead of calling him by his pet name Mannu. (His passport records his name as Analjit Singh a.k.a Mannu Mohan Singh. The addition to his passport was made in the 1970s when he was studying in the United States.)

He was more relaxed and friendly with Manjit. Analjit was like a handyman to his elder brother and his friends, running errands for them. In 1967, when Dr Singh returned from the United States, Analjit left for Doon School. His friends there included journalist Karan Thapar and Rajiv Khanna, grandson of hotelier Mohan Singh Oberoi. At school, Analjit excelled as a table tennis player and was a part of the school orchestra.

When in Delhi, Analjit would act as his father's secretary-cum-housekeeper at home. He would type out Bhai Mohan Singh's telegrams and try to find out why he was travelling abroad. Even at that time he was aware of his father's awesome network of contacts. 'Bhai Mohan Singh knew everybody and everybody knew Bhai Mohan Singh,' Analjit would recount decades later. Bhai Mohan Singh rarely had time for home and family. When Analjit was eighteen years old, Bhai Mohan Singh took him along on some of his overseas business trips to make up for the absence from home. On these visits, while Bhai Mohan Singh would be busy in business meetings during the day, Analjit was left on his own to explore and sightsee.

After passing out of Doon School in 1972, Analjit joined the Shri Ram College of Commerce in Delhi. Those were very good years for Analjit. Both his brothers had got married within a space of ten days. The whole family used to stay together, though a couple of years later, Dr Singh and Manjit moved to their new houses in the Aurangzeb Road complex. Analjit was particularly close to Dr Singh's wife, Nimmi. Whenever Dr Singh would go abroad, Analjit would be a devoted younger brother-in-law and look after her. In 1975, Analjit left for the United States to get an MBA degree. On his second visit home in December 1978, he was introduced to Neelu, a girl from Dehradun. He returned the next summer to get engaged to her and they were married on 30 December 1979, Bhai Mohan Singh's birthday.

Though Analjit worked with the Miami-based North

American Biologicals Inc. after completing his studies, Bhai Mohan Singh had different plans for him. Thus, the notice sent to Ranbaxy shareholders for the company's twentieth annual general meeting scheduled for 16 June 1981 at Mohali had an interesting item on the agenda—the appointment of Analjit as an executive in the senior cadre of the company from 1 June 1981.

Analjit made a lateral entry into the high-profile executive committee of Ranbaxy as director (projects), though he was not given a berth on the company's board of directors. This is when life took a u-turn for him.

The stupendous success of ampicillin, launched in 1977, required the company to go in for backward integration of its operations. Ranbaxy was still importing 6APA (6 amino-penicillic acid), the main ingredients of semi-synthetic penicillins, but it had started thinking in terms of manufacturing it as well. Though the 1977 annual report had mentioned that 'laboratory-scale work for the manufacture of 6APA has been completed and the process is now being up-scaled for commercial production', two years later, there was still no sign of the project being implemented.

By 1982, it was decided that the 6APA project would be Analjit's baby. Ranbaxy, in association with the Punjab State Industrial Development Corporation, promoted Max India Ltd, which put up a plant in the Hoshiarpur district of Punjab, a Centrally Notified Backward Area, for the manufacture of 6APA. The technology was provided by a Japanese company, Toyo Jozo Co. Ltd. It was seen as a major import substitution effort, potentially leading to substantial foreign exchange savings.

The 6APA project had become a matter of critical importance for Ranbaxy. The 1983 directors' report had noted that the company suffered heavily on account of the canalization of 6APA from January 1983. The government did not fix prices or arrange to procure stocks and release the intermediate to the industry till September 1983. The non-availability of 6APA affected the company's production of ampicillin.

Analjit had not been keen to join Ranbaxy after his return from the United States as he had seen Manjit floundering there. He was aware that Manjit had been trying out the hotels business but was getting very little support from his father and his eldest brother. Yet, because of his strong attachment to his parents and brothers, he wanted to work for the family. Within two days of his arrival in India, Analjit was ushered into Dr Singh's office at Okhla. Over the next hour or so, he was educated about 6APA and its critical importance for Ranbaxy's business of anti-infective drugs derived from semi-synthetic penicillin. At the end, he was told that nothing could be more appropriate for him to start his innings in business.

Less than a week after this meeting, Analjit found himself in a small cubicle as manager (new projects). It had a red phone, a red carpet and a red thermos, and a file marked 6APA lay on his table. He was assigned a secretary, Raghu, who eventually became like a member of the family. Analjit's salary was fixed at Rs 3,000 per month with no other financial emoluments.

Over the next year or so, Analjit realized that the 6APA project was fraught with difficulties. To begin with, production required an industrial licence. The government had already given out licences for all projected 6APA capacities. So there was no question of a new licence being issued. Second, technology to produce 6APA was not available in the country and it could only be procured from abroad. However, government rules of the time set a limit of $50,000 to acquire the technology. Third, Ranbaxy could not have imported penicillin, the raw material for 6APA, as it was on the negative list of imports. Analjit also realized that even if he did manage to get a special import licence for penicillin, the high customs duty would make the price of his 6APA three times the price of the ampicillin for which it was meant. The only option was to buy penicillin from the local producers—the public sector Hindustan Antibiotics Ltd and IDPL. But the quality of their penicillin was poor; instead of sparkling white, it was pale yellow in colour.

The first challenge before Analjit was to get a licence to produce 6APA. Here, he got Bhai Mohan Singh's help. The two argued with the licencing authorities that none of the companies which had been given 6APA licences had begun production. Moreover, as Ranbaxy was the country's largest producer of ampicillin, the project was all the more critical for it. Finally, the government relented and a licence was given to Analjit. By then, Analjit had also identified Toyo Jozo as a technology partner. To implement the project, he formed a new company called Max India. The M in Max stood for Bhai Mohan Singh, A for Avtar Kaur and X for all others.

But the biggest challenge was still awaiting Analjit. The cost of the 6APA venture was estimated at around Rs 5 crore. As he had no personal wealth, Analjit had no option but to ask the family and Ranbaxy to bankroll the project. To his surprise, he was told that the family would not invest more than Rs 25 lakh in the project, and Dr Singh told him that Ranbaxy would not put in more than Rs 40 lakh. That left a yawning gap in finances. Undaunted, Analjit persevered with the project, taking personal loans to bridge the equity gap. The 6APA plant was set up at Taonsa. It took Analjit almost eighteen years after Max India started in 1985 to repay the loans he had taken. The sum of Rs 65 lakh is the only financial help from the family or Ranbaxy that Analjit received in his life.

Having been in the pharmaceutical business for over fifteen years, Dr Singh could not have been unaware of the pitfalls in the project. Then why did he push his brother into the project knowing that he had no work experience in India? The only explanation Analjit could come up with was that Dr Singh did all this to toughen his youngest brother. Or did Dr Singh not want his brother to succeed? After all, Manjit too had not been able to realize his dream of building a hotel because of stiff resistance from Dr Singh. Nobody doubted the fact that the hotel project would definitely have come about if Dr Singh had thrown his weight behind it.

More importantly, why did Bhai Mohan Singh not come out in support of Analjit, especially when it came to funding the 6APA venture? In his eyes, his eldest son, who was in the process of single-handedly turning around the fortunes of Ranbaxy, could do no wrong.

In spite of the odds stacked against him, Analjit pressed on. He introduced certain technical changes in the 6APA plant which resulted in considerable productivity improvement. Two years later, in 1987, he had added a 7ADCA (7-aminodeacetoxycephalosporanic acid) unit to the plant. 7ADCA is a key intermediate for the production of cephalexin, cefradine and other cephalosporins. This drove the profitability of the company.

Though he got little support from the family, Analjit was fortunate to have a loyal band of executives working for him, led by Ashwani Windlass. By the end of his innings at Max India, Windlass came to be known as one of the finest strategists in the corporate world. Windlass had started his career in 1978 as a management trainee with Delhi-based DCM Ltd. In 1981, he had joined Ranbaxy's finance department. Soon he was attached to Analjit for the 6APA project. When Max India was formed in 1984, he was made the company's CFO at just twenty-seven years of age. Apart from looking after the finances of Max India, he was soon advising Analjit on new business possibilities, given the tough nature of the 6APA business.

One business on Analjit and Windlass's shortlist was electronics. Once again, the proposal met with a stiff resistance from the family, which argued that any investment outside pharmaceuticals would be suicidal. Instead of getting bogged down by criticism, Analjit decided to go ahead on his own. As a foray into electronics would require substantial investments, he decided to get into duty-free trading which would generate capital for the electronics venture. He floated a company called Dove Corporation in the mid-1980s, which was soon representing over twenty famous liquor and fashion brands in India's duty-free shops. Once it had started generating profits, the company got into distribution of equipment and components for the electronics industry.

The next business Max India got into was BOPP (Biaxially Oriented Polypropylene) films. Analjit and Windlass were convinced that as the Indian economy grew, demand for synthetic packaging material would also go up. Their projections were accurate. When the economy opened up, BOPP films became hugely popular and the business raked in profits for Analjit for many years to come. This was not the first time that the two were able to look beyond the immediate future. This time also, Analjit was told that he would not get any financial support from the family and that he would have to fend for himself. Analjit had floated a new company called Maxxon India in 1992. The cost of the project was estimated at Rs 30 crore. With investors reluctant to put their money into a greenfield venture, Analjit and Windlass devised an issue of convertible bonds in 1993. Investors would get a fixed return till the project materialized, after which they could convert the bonds into equity shares.

At the time when Maxxon was on the drawing board, the family assets were divided between the three brothers. Whatever little hopes Analjit had of receiving support from the family got dashed in 1989. Things took a turn for the worse soon.

*

Ranbaxy was the largest buyer of 6APA and 7ADCA in the Indian market, accounting for around 30 per cent of the total production in the country. Max India got almost 60 per cent of its business from Ranbaxy. In 1991, Ranbaxy pulled the rug from under Max India's feet when it set up its own 7ADCA unit at Mohali. Ranbaxy was facing a pressure on cephalosporin prices as several companies abroad, including Antibioticos in Spain, Dobfar in Italy, Royal Gist-Brocades (GB) in The Netherlands and a handful of Indian companies like Lupin and later Orchid had gone in for backward integration and set up 7ADCA facilities. Ranbaxy's competitiveness in cephalosporins was under threat and the only way to restore profitability was to manufacture its own 7ADCA. Max India was plunged into a severe financial crisis. Analjit charged his brother of reneging on his commitment to support Max India. But Dr Singh refused to budge. Analjit had no choice but to bring the profitable Dove Corporation within the Max India fold. It was made a division of the company and re-christened Max Electronics.

Meanwhile, the BOPP films business also started totting up losses. The 1991 Gulf War had caused raw material prices to rise sharply. At the same time, as the economy was going through a slump, there was intense competition at home resulting in prices being slashed. Maxxon had to function with another handicap: while rivals like Cosmo Films with its unit at Aurangabad and Gujarat Propack in Gujarat were close to the ports, its unit was located in Punjab, requiring huge investments in logistics. A stage was reached in 1991 when bankruptcy was staring at Maxxon.

Once again, Windlass showed the way out. He proposed a reverse merger of Max India into Maxxon. This would give Maxxon a new lease of life. The reverse merger was done in 1993 and Maxxon was subsequently renamed Max India. Still, the struggle was far from over for Analjit. Relations between the two brothers only deteriorated in the days to come.

*

GB or Royal Gist-Brocades had emerged as the world's leading producer of penicillin and its derivatives like 6APA and 7ADCA over the years. It knew that it needed to locate cheaper sources of supply of 6APA, if it wanted to maintain its leadership position in the long run. It was facing competition from Max in the European markets. GB was selling 6APA at as high a price as $400 per kg. Once Max entered the market, it was forced to drop its price to $150 per kg. Hence, it began to scout for opportunities in India. It spoke to a number of companies, including Ranbaxy, but finally tied up with Max in 1994. The 6APA and 7ADCA business was now parked in a new company called Max GB, in which both the partners held a 50 per cent stake.

More importantly, from Analjit's point of view, the joint venture agreement said that Max GB would pay Max India Rs 6 crore a year as 'rights to use' fees for the USFDA approved 6APA and 7ADCA plant at Bhai Mohan Singh Nagar. It was a great deal for Analjit. He had not given up control of the business and had ensured that Rs 6 crore got added on to Max India's bottom line every year.

Max India, by now, had emerged as the largest buyer of penicillin in the country. While it was procuring 30 per cent of its requirement locally from Hindustan Antibiotics, it was importing the remaining 70 per cent. It only made sense for Max India to get into penicillin production in order to control costs and get a better grip on the quality of its products. Meanwhile, by 1989, it had become clear to the government that the policy of restricting the production of penicillin to the public sector had lost its relevance. It thus handed out almost a dozen licences to the private sector, including one each to Max India and Ranbaxy.

Analjit first proposed a three-way joint venture to produce penicillin between Max India, Ranbaxy and Antibioticos. But Ranbaxy was cold to the proposal and the venture did not materialize. Ranbaxy had actually decided against getting into penicillin after carefully studying the matter. One, the prices were slated to fall with new capacities coming up. Two, Ranbaxy by now had embarked on an ambitious programme for global expansion and saw little merit in investing in a penicillin plant at the time.

Around the same time, Hindustan Antibiotics realized that it needed to upgrade its penicillin facility in order to survive once private sector players got into production. It approached GB for help, which said that all its business in India would be carried out by Max GB. This brought Max India in touch with Hindustan Antibiotics.

Analjit had now come to realize that a greenfield penicillin venture could be very expensive. The cost of putting up a new plant of a decent size was estimated at nothing less than Rs 150 crore. Given the imminent fall in global penicillin prices, it did not make sense to invest large sums of money in new plant and machinery. Again, Analjit proposed something that was not on anybody's radar screen: a joint venture with Hindustan Antibiotics to take over its penicillin facility. This was much before the country had even started thinking in terms of divesting the government's stake in the public sector. Analjit threw a sweetener into the deal and said that the joint venture company would pay Hindustan Antibiotics a sum of Rs 17 crore every year for using its facility. He also assured that he would double the production of penicillin from the facility and reduce costs by half without making any significant investments.

Hindustan Antibiotics could not have asked for a better deal. It would get GB technology to upgrade its facility and Rs 17 crore every year as lease rental, all without making any financial commitment. All hurdles appeared to have been cleared for the formation of the fifty-fifty joint venture, Hindustan Max GB Ltd. Analjit, who was then living in a suite in Claridges Hotel because his house was being renovated, was confident that the joint venture had come through. After a particularly fruitful meeting with the government, he had even uncorked a bottle of champagne for his close friends. He had not anticipated the unpleasant turn the whole affair was set to take.

Two days after Max GB and Hindustan Antibiotics signed the agreement in 1995, Torrent moved a public interest litigation (PIL) in the Delhi High Court alleging that the deal lacked transparency. As Hindustan Antibiotics was a public sector undertaking, it should have invited tenders for selecting a partner rather than strike a deal privately, the PIL said. Soon, Chennai-based Spic Pharmaceuticals and Delhi-based JK Pharmaceuticals too had moved similar PILs and the Delhi High Court decided to club the three petitions into one.

All the three applicants had committed investments in excess of Rs 150 crore each for new penicillin plants. Torrent had even raised money from the market for the venture. The Max GB–Hindustan Antibiotics deal put a question mark on these projects as, with high interest rates prevailing at that time and depreciation, these companies would never be able to match the prices of the joint venture.

Soon the media was full of reports that the government had sold out to Max India and GB. The matter came up before the Parliamentary Standing Committee on chemicals. The smear campaign against Analjit and Hindustan Antibiotics managing director, A.K. Basu, had begun. Analjit had reasons to believe that the campaign against him was being orchestrated by Ranbaxy. His close aides would say that several unsigned notes that were circulated those days, ostensibly in public interest, originated from Ranbaxy. Several such faxes were found to bear the Ranbaxy address. Ranbaxy, on its part, denied any involvement. But that didn't matter as Analjit was convinced of its involvement. 'My brother loved to push a chilli up my back every day,' Analjit would recount many years later.

The perfect gentleman that he was, Analjit still refrained from badmouthing his brother in public. Yet, he decided to hit back. Operating out of his suite in Claridges, his team soon joined the trial by media. Journalists covering the slugfest had a field day.

Analjit and Windlass had done their homework quite well. All decisions related to the deal were properly documented. The final court verdict went in their favour and Hindustan Max GB commenced operations. Still, the mudslinging and the court battles took their toll on Analjit. He aged dramatically during those years, worry lines marking his otherwise youthful face. He became more spiritual, placing immense faith on divine justice.

Analjit's aides from those days insist that Ranbaxy's ire had been provoked due to another factor. Max was looking at spreading its wings in pharmaceuticals beyond 6APA and 7ADCA. In the family settlement, Max India had acquired the Okhla factory complete with its 600 workers. On its sixth founder's day celebrations in 1991, it gave awards to employees of the Okhla factory for completing twenty-five years of service! Still, by the early-1990s, Analjit was able to trim the workforce substantially through voluntary separation schemes. He now started making a wide range of formulations here. He quickly became a fairly large player in generic medicine. He had also launched a publicity campaign, 'Take Good Care of Your Body', in the media, which was well received in the medical fraternity. Next on the cards was a bulk drugs plant in the southern state of Karnataka.

The big moment came when Max India tied up with United States-based Upjohn Co. Ltd for distributing its products in the country. It went on to launch Upjohn's controversial injectible contraceptive for women, Depo-Provera, in the country. The product had received USFDA's clearance only a year earlier. The launch caused an uproar, especially amongst women's rights activists, but the company went ahead.

Meanwhile, the relationship between the brothers had touched a new low. To his close aides Analjit would call Dr Singh cold and calculating, devoid of any emotion. But as a businessman, he was always full of respect for Dr Singh. 'Ranbaxy had an unbeatable team: Bhai Mohan Singh built the brand, Dr Singh gave the vision and corporate governance and Brar is the best in execution,' he said of Ranbaxy's success years later. When Dr Singh fell ill, he told his close aides that both companies could have achieved so much more had the two brothers decided to work together.

Analjit gradually exited from the pharmaceuticals business. He ceded a controlling stake to GB in Max GB (this also took away Hindustan Max GB away from him), sold the formulations business, including brands and stock-in-trade to Rhône-Poulenc and finally sold the bulk drugs plant to Delhi-based Jubilant Organosys (earlier known as Vam Organics) promoted by Shyam and Hari Bhartiya. The Bhartiyas engaged Jag Mohan Khanna, the former research and development chief of Ranbaxy, to steer their pharmaceuticals business. Analjit was to find his riches elsewhere.

*

By the late 1980s, Dove Corporation (before it became Max Electronics) was supplying components to consumer electronics companies, the defence services and a host of telecommunication companies like EPABX system manufacturers and the government's Centre for Development of Telematics (C-DOT). Almost 60 per cent of the business came from the telecom companies.

Windlass was convinced that India was headed for a telecom revolution. Thus, in 1991, much before the government came out with its National Telecom Policy, Max India, along with United States-based telecom major Motorola and Mumbai-based Arya Communications, a distributor of Motorola components, applied for a nation-wide paging licence. It was the first case to come up before the newly-formed Foreign Investment Promotion Board (FIPB). Radio paging had taken the world by storm in the late 1980s. Much before anybody else could even think of it, Max India had sought government permission to bring the service to India.

However, Analjit and Windlass realized that, the world over, telecom was a services business and they had tied up with Motorola, an equipment manufacturer. If Max India had to enter the sector, it would have to tie up with a telecom service provider. Thus began Max India's search for a telecom partner. In the end, it was Motorola that helped Max India sign up with Li Ka-shing of Hong Kong.

*

Born in 1928, Li Ka-shing was the chairman of Cheung Kong (Holdings) Ltd and Hutchison Whampoa Ltd. Li Ka-shing had founded Cheung Kong Industries in 1950, which started as a plastics manufacturer and later evolved into a property investment company. The group acquired Hutchison Whampoa in 1979.

By 2003, Cheung Kong Group's business straddled such diverse areas as property development and investment, real estate and estate management, hotels, telecommunications and e-commerce, finance and investment, retail and manufacturing, ports and related services, energy, infrastructure projects and materials, media, and biotechnology. Based in Hong Kong, the combined group ranks among the top 100 corporations in the world.

Hutchison Whampoa's origins can be traced to 1828 when a small dispensary company called A.S. Watson opened in the Guangzhou province of China. By 1841, it expanded its operations to Hong Kong. In 1863, the Hongkong and Whampoa Dock Company (HWD) was established to acquire docks and repair yards at Whampoa, on the Pearl river in China, and at the then newly-constructed dry docks at Aberdeen on Hong Kong Island.

In the late 1800s, a young Briton by the name of John Duflon Hutchison, who had come to Hong Kong, set up the John D. Hutchison and Company Ltd, laying the foundation of the Hutchison business empire. In the 1960s, Hutchison International Ltd began an acquisition programme, which gave it control of, among others, HWD. Hutchison Whampoa Ltd was born in 1977 as a result of a merger between the two companies. In January 1978, Hutchison Whampoa Ltd became a listed company in Hong Kong. In 1979, Li Ka-shing acquired a substantial shareholding in the company from the Hongkong and Shanghai Bank, thus becoming the first Chinese to take control of a British-style 'hong' (business empire). Li Ka-shing was amongst the first to spot the opportunity in cellular services. In 1985, he ventured into cellular telephony and the Hutchison Telephone Company Ltd was established to launch Hong Kong's first cellular mobile telephone system. In 1989, Hutchison Telecom entered the British and Australian mobile telecommunications markets.

Meanwhile, the Indian government had opened up cellular services, inviting bids for the four metros of Mumbai, Delhi, Chennai and Kolkata. Hutchison and Max India officials got together to draft their bid document. Bidders were required to give the broad parameters of their proposed service, on the basis of which the government would award the circles. Nobody knew what weight the government would assign to the various parameters. While the bid document was being prepared, Windlass insisted that it be mentioned that consumers would be charged zero rental. It so happened the government had decided to give maximum weightage to rentals. As a result, when the bids were opened, Hutchison Max was right on top with a score of ninety-two out of 100. It was on its way to get a licence to operate cellular services in Mumbai, the commercial capital of India.

However, owing to a slight oversight in the bid document, Hutchison Max was disqualified. But the company went to the courts and got a favourable judgment. The day after the judgment, Mumbai woke up to thirty-one hoardings put up at prime locations by Hutchison Max, saying 'Hello Bombay'.

Cellular telephony is a capital-intensive business. The choice before Analjit was to keep on pumping money or encash his stake. In 1997, on Janmashtami, the day Hindus celebrate the birth of Lord Krishna, Analjit decided on the latter course of action. The divestment exercise was aptly named Project Krishna. In April 1998, Max India offloaded 41 per cent of its stake in the company to its joint venture partner for Rs 549 crore. Analjit's business finally was flush with funds.

Once the money from the Hutchison deal was in the coffers of Max India, Analjit decided to just relax for the next six months. That is the time Windlass, his trusted aide, who did not want to miss out on the action in telecom, decided to leave Max, though he continued to serve on its board of directors. The question confronting Singh was, what next?

At that time, all Singh knew was that he had had enough of manufacturing and chasing bureaucrats. 'I knew the name of every guard in Shastri Bhawan. With the telecom venture, the babus in Sanchar Bhawan (the headquarters of the Department of Telecom) got added to the list. *Pagal kar diya tha* (they drove me mad),' Singh would recall. To help him make up his mind, the consultancy firm Mckinsey was called on board. A Mckinsey executive asked Analjit to write his obituary in 800 words—what did he want to be remembered as. The trick worked. Analjit wrote the obituary and, at the end of it, knew what he wanted to do. 'I want to make Max the country's most admired company in service excellence. I want to do what Naresh Goel has done with Jet (Airways) or what the Oberois have done (in the hotels business),' Singh told himself.

He identified three areas of growth: healthcare delivery, life insurance and information technology. The vision was further narrowed to healthcare and life insurance by 2002. In-between, he also made a foray into clinical research. He began by setting up three companies to this effect: Neeman Medical International Plc in the United Kingdom, Neeman Medical International Inc. in the United States and Neeman Asia Ltd in India. In 2001, Max India acquired a 75 per cent stake in Instituto Costarricense De Investigaciones Clinicas, a clinical research firm based at San José, Costa Rica, at a cost of $6.5 million. This company had fifty-three people on its rolls and its list of clients included Pfizer, Eli Lilly, Roche, Johnson & Johnson and GSK. The acquisition was to become a springboard for an entry in the clinical research business in Latin America.

Analjit also felt that Max India required a new corporate identity. Thus was born the new logo of Max India—a blue earthen lamp with a saffron flame accompanying the lettering, Max. The saffron flame was a symbol of the country's spirituality and represents power, strength and knowledge.

*

Still, Analjit remained unhappy and resentful with the family situation. Over the years, he became a votary of keeping families away from business. At the Young Presidents' Organization, he constantly spoke on how joint families destroy wealth.

Sometime in the late 1990s, when his son, Vir, broached the topic of joining the family business, Analjit asked him to fetch the atlas. With the family huddled round it, he told Vir: 'Son, there is this whole world outside and all you want to do is work with Papa?'

6

The Cefaclor Challenge

In May 1876, Col. Eli Lilly, a thirty-eight-year-old American chemist, frustrated with the quality of medicine being sold in the United States at the time, set up a company called Eli Lilly at Indianapolis. His aim was to provide medicines of a consistent quality. He had also decided that these medicines would be sold only through doctors and not through shamans and quacks as was common in those days.

Although his business was successful, Col. Lilly wasn't satisfied with the traditional methods of quality testing. In 1886, he hired a young chemist as a full-time scientist, and entrusted him with the task of using and improving upon the newest techniques of quality evaluation. Together, they laid the foundation for Eli Lilly's research and development programme which first concentrated on improving the quality of existing products and later expanded to include the discovery and development of new and better pharmaceuticals.

Over the years, Eli Lilly came out with a string of revolutionary products. In the 1920s, its researchers collaborated with Frederick Banting and Charles Best of the University of Toronto to isolate and purify insulin for the treatment of diabetes, then a fatal disease with no effective treatment options. The work resulted in Eli Lilly's introduction of Iletin in 1923, the world's first commercially available insulin product.

In the 1960s, Eli Lilly launched the first of a long line of oral and injectible antibiotics in a new class called cephalosporins. Over the next two decades, the company pioneered important chemical breakthroughs that allowed the large-scale production of these antibiotics, which included cephalexin under the brand name Keflex and cefazolin sodium under the brand name Kefzol. In the late-1970s, it developed cefaclor, a member of the cephalosporin family, and launched it under the brand name Ceclor. Ceclor went on to become the world's top-selling oral antibiotic. Unknown to Eli Lilly, a little-known Indian company operating out of a cramped commercial district in New Delhi was all set to upset its monopoly of cefaclor.

*

Dr Singh had developed a global vision very early in his career. He would share it, way back in the mid-1970s, with his close friends like P.D. Sheth and Bimal Raizada, though they refused to take him seriously. He would often say that there was nothing that Indian scientists could not achieve if they got proper guidance. He had seen Indian scientists at work in the United States during his student days and this convinced him that they were comparable with the best in the world. Dr Singh realized this much before Indians were to swamp pharmaceutical research in the United States. When he died in 1999, almost 15 per cent of those engaged in pharmaceutical research in that country were of Indian origin.

Dr Singh was also amongst the first in the Indian

pharmaceutical business to realize that since the country accounted for only 1.2 per cent of the world pharmaceutical market, a viable business model—not restricted by the size of the local market—would have to base itself on global markets. With this in view, Ranbaxy took the pioneering step of exporting bulk drugs from India in 1987-88, even though the margins in the export business were not high. But the company knew that in order to drive long-term growth, it would have to make such sacrifices.

Dr Singh had his sights trained on the United States. Ranbaxy did have manufacturing operations in Nigeria, Malaysia, Thailand and China by then, but these ventures were small. Moreover, these countries were on the fringes of the world pharmaceutical market. Going truly global has always meant a presence in the United States, which accounts for almost half the world market.

By the late-1980s, the entire Ranbaxy brass had started talking in hushed tones about exporting to the United States. It had come to the company's notice that the United States patent on cephalexin had expired in 1987. Ranbaxy was the leading cephalexin player in India at that time; its brand, Sporidex, was the market leader. It was time to make the dream of selling in the United States come true.

Tentative inquiries were made in the United States about whether or not Indian drug companies could sell there. Brar travelled to the United States to get a feel of the market. After meeting a host of companies there, including Barr Pharmaceuticals, Stein Pharmaceuticals and Duramed Pharmaceuticals, he came to the conclusion that the company would not be able to upgrade itself even in the next four to five years in terms of product quality, manufacturing infrastructure, regulatory compliance and availability of surplus cash to venture into the American market. His recommendations were in sharp contrast to the expectations that had built up. There was a sense of loss within the company. The American dream, which for a moment had looked within reach, was once again rendered unachievable. In hindsight, it was a wise decision on Brar's part. His report resulted in the company embarking on a slow but steady exercise to upgrade its various systems with an eye on the United States market.

After ampicillin, Ranbaxy had entered the cephalosporin market where its Sporidex brand had done extremely well. As cephalosporins were expected to outlast ampicillin, the company decided to focus on this category of drugs and by the mid-1980s had pinpointed cefaclor for development. It was a very big product with global sales of $1.4 billion. Eli Lilly had the patent rights till 1992 and had announced that it would continue with its franchise for the drug. If Ranbaxy could develop a non-infringing method to develop the drug, it could show to the world that it had the inherent capabilities required for developing complex products.

That was easier said than done. Eli Lilly had sixty-odd process patents, effectively blocking any new method of producing the drug. Companies like Roche, Biochem, Opus and Dobfar had been attempting to develop a generic version of the drug for quite sometime but with no success. Eli Lilly was confident that it would face no competition on cefaclor. Jag Mohan Khanna and his band of scientists at Ranbaxy proved it wrong.

*

Khanna had joined Ranbaxy in 1979 as head of chemical research after Gopinath left. After working at the Central Drug Research Institute (CDRI), Lucknow, for nine years, where he did his Ph.D under Dr Nitya Nand, Khanna left for the United States, where he worked for the next six years—three years in Ohio State University and three years with Riker Pharma, a 3M company in California. But his love for the country brought him back to India. He surrendered his Green Card and started searching for a job.

He was unwilling to join a government organization because of the poor financial remuneration and lack of appreciation of good work. Through his friends, Khanna came to know that Ranbaxy was looking for somebody with a background in pharmaceutical chemistry and that the company was trying hard to develop new process technologies, especially in anti-infectives. He called Dr Singh and was soon on the company's rolls as chemical research manager, heading a team of five scientists. (When Khanna left the company in 2002, there were 750 scientists working under him. Thanks to the string of successes in research and development starting with cefaclor, Khanna went on to join the Ranbaxy board. When he reached the retirement age in 2000, Ranbaxy gave him two extensions of one year each.)

Khanna soon realized that very few people were willing to join Ranbaxy because of its reputation of being an arrogant company. However, he persevered and, over the next few years, was instrumental in developing a number of new products for Ranbaxy. Sometime in 1989, he was given the brief to develop cefaclor. This was Khanna's toughest challenge so far. Given the complexity of the molecule, his first task was to put together a crack team for the project. As sufficient in-house talent was not available, he had to get somebody from outside. He finally recruited Yatinder Kumar as group leader for the project.

*

Kumar had also done his Ph.D in medicinal chemistry under Dr Nitya Nand at the CDRI. It was then that Astra, the Swedish pharmaceutical company, offered him a job for one year. Kumar agreed and went to the Astra headquarters on the outskirts of Stockholm to take up the position of 'guest scientist' in the company's central nervous system department. Within no time he had impressed the Swedes so much that he was offered a permanent position. He stayed on at Astra for five years. But, unhappy with the high tax rates in Sweden, he shifted to the United States in mid-1983 and joined the University of Michigan, Ann Arbor—the same university where Dr Singh had studied.

However, Kumar started yearning for his homeland. He was ambitious but felt that it would be difficult for him to reach the top in a foreign country. In 1988, Khanna approached him with an offer to work for Ranbaxy on the cefaclor project. Though the compensation offered by Ranbaxy was not at par with what he was currently getting, Khanna promised to give him a free hand at work and a laboratory comparable to one in the United States. Though Kumar had applied for a Green Card for permanent residence in the United States, he packed his bags and returned to India with his family.

However, once he started working at the cramped Ranbaxy laboratory at Okhla, Kumar was disillusioned soon. Nothing in the company's infrastructure met his expectations. As he had a standing offer from his boss at the University of Michigan, Ann Arbor, Dr Larry Townsend, to come back in case of any problem, Kumar decided to return to the United States within one year. But the United States embassy denied him a visa and Kumar was left with no option but to stay back. With the United States option closed, he applied himself to the cefaclor project with renewed vigour.

It was an uphill task. Cefaclor was a delicate molecule to handle and it would often break. The process was hazardous as it used ozone, which is highly explosive, and the scale-up (migration from laboratory to factory for production) was complicated. Eli Lilly was only too aware of the complexities and was confident that nobody else, least of all an unheard of company in India, would be able to develop the molecule. It took Kumar and his team a year and a half to understand the molecule. And it took another year for the scale-up at Ranbaxy's Mohali plant. But at the end, by 1991, it had developed a non-infringing process to make cefaclor. Dr Singh was elated. Khanna and Kumar were given citations for their scientific work. Dr Singh also gave Kumar Rs 5,000 and introduced him to Bhai Mohan Singh.

In 1991, with just 1–2 gm of cefaclor synthesized in its laboratories, the company took the big decision to go ahead and set up a production line for cefaclor. It was a race against time for Ranbaxy. Its product had to be ready once the patent expired in 1992. It made an investment of around Rs 40 crore to set up its cefaclor facility. It was the first amongst the several bold steps that Ranbaxy was to make. At the time of making this investment in 1991-92, Ranbaxy had a turnover of Rs 334.05 crore, a net profit of Rs 16.47 crore and a net worth of only Rs 63.04 crore. To commit such a large investment on a single product was quite a risk. Yet, the company went ahead with it and the gamble paid off.

Once the plant was ready, Dr Singh and Brar realized that the company was too small to sell the drug in the United States on its own. The interests of the company, they felt, would be served best by entering into a tie-up with Eli Lilly to sell advanced intermediates of the product. Soon, Brar was in the United States to initiate negotiations with Eli Lilly. But, unlike on his last visit, Brar was negotiating from a position of strength this time. Eli Lilly could not afford to ignore Ranbaxy any more.

When Ranbaxy's process for the production of cefaclor was published, Eli Lilly could find nothing to challenge it in the courts. The only alternative left for it was to form some kind of a relationship with Ranbaxy. It then invited Ranbaxy's core cefaclor team—Khanna, Kumar and Dr Naresh Kumar (the chemical research manager who was also an alumnus of CDRI)—to the United States for discussions on the process technology developed by them.

The team was hosted by, among others, Sydney Taurel,

the future Eli Lilly chairman and CEO. Born a Spanish citizen in Casablanca, Morocco, Taurel, who became an American citizen in November 1995, studied first in France and then received an MBA from Columbia University in 1971. He joined Eli Lilly International Corporation the same year as a marketing associate and held various positions in the company's offices in South America, Europe and the United Kingdom, before returning to Indianapolis in 1986 as president of Eli Lilly International Corporation. In 1991, when the Ranbaxy bombshell exploded, he had just been appointed executive vice-president of the pharmaceutical division of Eli Lilly and co-opted into the company's board of directors.

The meetings between Eli Lilly and Ranbaxy's team of scientists went off well and, in November 1991, Brar got the first indications that the two companies could get into a sourcing agreement for cefaclor. Everybody was thrilled. In early-1992, Eli Lilly finally dispatched a team to India to inspect Ranbaxy's facilities, especially the cefaclor production lines. Though the lines were not fully ready, Ranbaxy technicians were able to provide a demonstration. The Eli Lilly team went back convinced.

When Ranbaxy had first developed cefaclor using its own processes, there were doubts whether Eli Lilly would talk to the company at all. So when Eli Lilly came to India, discreet hints were dropped that Ranbaxy could flood the unregulated markets with its version of cefaclor. This could have clinched the deal with Eli Lilly. Several American and European pharmaceutical companies had realized by now that Ranbaxy had the capabilities to erode their profitability in unregulated markets by launching cheaper clones of drugs. There was also the danger that once Ranbaxy's cheaper cefaclor was available in the market, some governments could crack down on Eli Lilly for charging very high prices.

Eli Lilly complimented Ranbaxy's scientists on their achievement, and offered to buy out Ranbaxy's entire production of cefaclor. Since Ranbaxy had developed cefaclor using a different process, Eli Lilly would not buy the final output as it would be perceived in the market as a different product. So it offered to buy the penultimate product—one step short of cefaclor—and do the final process itself. Initially, the orders were small. But once the Ranbaxy cefaclor was accepted in the market, the size of the orders from Eli Lilly went up significantly.

This gave the biggest boost ever to Ranbaxy's profits. Reserving for itself the rights for markets where there were no patents, Ranbaxy agreed to sell its entire cefaclor production of 40 tonnes per annum to Eli Lilly at $2,000 per kg, while its cost of production was a little over $500 per kg. In other words, the company made a profit of approximately $1,450 on every kilogram of cefaclor it sold to Eli Lilly.

More importantly, cefaclor showed to the world that Ranbaxy was capable of mastering complex technologies. It was well known at that time that a clutch of generic producers had been trying very hard to develop a non-infringing process to develop cefaclor. But it was Ranbaxy which first came out with the product.

The cefaclor success galvanized Ranbaxy into drawing up big plans for the future. Dr Singh now had the financial wherewithal to realize his long-cherished dream of making Ranbaxy a global pharmaceutical company. Though he would seldom talk about his dream before the cefaclor success, his close friends knew that he had nurtured such ambitions from the day he joined Ranbaxy.

In 1992-93, Ranbaxy entered into an alliance with Eli Lilly to float a joint venture company in India called Eli Lilly Ranbaxy Ltd to produce and market select products from the Eli Lilly portfolio. On 24 January 1995, Ranbaxy signed a global alliance agreement with Eli Lilly for marketing pharmaceutical products in the United States and other markets. Soon afterwards, the two companies signed two agreements on 2 June 1995 for setting up two more joint ventures, one in India and the other in the United States. They would be equal partners in these ventures. The Indian joint venture was for research, development and manufacturing of generic products; extension of current Eli Lilly and Ranbaxy products; and for development of new products of both companies. For this purpose, a new company called Ranbaxy Lilly Company was incorporated. The joint venture in the United States was to focus on marketing of products from the Indian joint venture as well as other select Ranbaxy and Eli Lilly products. This company was called Lilly Ranbaxy Pharmaceuticals LLC and was incorporated in the state of Indiana.

There was another reason for Eli Lilly to forge an alliance with Ranbaxy. In the early-1990s, when Bill Clinton was serving his first term as the President of the United States, his wife, Hillary, had started a campaign for health reforms in the country. It was found that a large portion of the aged population in the country did not have insurance cover, which put expensive medicines beyond their reach. The Clinton Administration decided to bring medicines to these underprivileged classes by encouraging the production of cheap generics.

This sent most research-based companies searching for a partner, which would catapult them straightaway into the generics space, though a few like the Swiss company Novartis set up their own generics business in the form of Geneva Pharmaceuticals. Apart from securing a piece of the business, most of these companies also wanted to present their humanitarian face to the Clinton Administration. Similar considerations had driven Eli Lilly to propose the three joint ventures with Ranbaxy. The timing of the cefaclor development couldn't have been better for Ranbaxy.

The alliance was like Goliath and David coming together. By end-2002, while Ranbaxy was still short of reporting a turnover of $1 billion, Eli Lilly's turnover was in excess of

$11 billion. Its expenditure on research and development during the year was $2.15 billion. Of the 43,000 people working for Eli Lilly worldwide across 146 countries, as many as 8,300 were involved in research and development.

*

Cefaclor proved to be the turning point for Ranbaxy. With this one product, it had arrived on the world pharmaceutical stage. Never before had an Indian pharmaceutical company synthesized such a complex product. As a result, many companies in the West, which had so far been cold to Ranbaxy, dismissing it as a company doing copies of simple drugs, started looking at it with renewed respect.

Several American drug companies now started talking to Ranbaxy for the supply of generic medicines. Notable amongst these were Biocraft Laboratories, Schein Pharmaceuticals and Barr Laboratories. Ranbaxy later signed a deal with Schein for the supply of ranitidine, Glaxo's blockbuster drug which had gone off-patent. It also entered into a tie-up with Barr for the supply of Cefadroxil Hemihydrate. Subsequently, Dobfar, which had tried to develop cefaclor on its own, started sourcing it from Ranbaxy. Later, the tie-up was expanded to other products as well.

More important, the cefaclor success gave research and development its rightful place within Ranbaxy. So far, it had been functioning out of a cramped laboratory at the Okhla office. Dr Singh now decided that the research and development team needed more space with better equipment and testing facilities. Also, the Okhla factory had gone to Analjit in the 1989 split. Dr Singh quickly located a piece of land at Gurgaon, on the outskirts of Delhi, to put up the new research and development unit. The equipment for the laboratory was personally chosen by Khanna, who was also instrumental in designing the layout. In the end, the company put together a world-class laboratory for its scientists. In a few short years, Ranbaxy added a second unit close to the first laboratory. By 2002, Ranbaxy was again running out of space for research and development. It then decided to add a third unit.

Over the years, Ranbaxy's scientists grew from developing new process technologies to the discovery of new chemical entities and new drug delivery systems. From modest beginnings, the company's research and development budget had crossed Rs 192 crore by 2002.

7

The Bitter Separation

It was called the Aurangzeb syndrome. Mughal emperor Aurangzeb had seized the kingdom after a bloody conflict with his father, Shahjahan, and his brothers. Shahjahan had been imprisoned in the Red Fort of Agra and he died in captivity.

In the 1980s, there had been several instances of bitter corporate rifts in India, where business associates had almost come to blows with each other. There were also cases of cousins and brothers at each other's throats. But never had a son risen against his father. However, in the early 1990s, two such family spats stunned the corporate world.

The first was between Raunaq Singh of the Delhi-based Apollo Tyres and his son Onkar Singh Kanwar. Raunaq Singh had risen from humble origins in pre-Partition Punjab. After Partition, he moved to Delhi and built up a steel tubes business brick by brick. He joined the big league in the mid-1970s when he ventured into the tyres business with Apollo Tyres. In the next few years, his son turned it into one of the country's premier tyre companies, getting Continental AG of Germany as a technology partner. Father and son got into a confrontation over the control of Apollo Tyres, which had emerged as the family's cash cow by the late-1980s. The fight was soon out in the open and there was much mudslinging from both sides. Finally, Raunaq Singh was ousted from the company and Onkar Singh Kanwar gained full control of Apollo Tyres.

However, in terms of sheer unpleasantness, this fight was nothing when compared to the one between Bhai Mohan Singh and Dr Singh. It generated more sadness, bitterness and pain than any other family separation in India Inc.

Even Ranbaxy insiders and those who knew the family well were taken by surprise. After all, Dr Singh was Bhai Mohan Singh's favourite son, a fact he made no secret of. In an article published in the *Tribune* of Chandigarh in 1984, Bhai Mohan Singh was quoted as saying: 'I feel particularly blessed that I have a brilliant son who has done in two years, against the three years taken by others, his Ph.D in pharmacy from a US university. He has been particularly helpful to me in the launching of one unit of our company in Nigeria and another in Malaysia.' Though the newspaper called it 'more an acknowledgement of fact than an expression of parental pride', everybody knew who was the apple of Bhai Mohan Singh's eye.

Bhai Mohan Singh was particularly proud of his son's academic achievements—nobody in his family or in his circle of friends could boast of such educational qualifications. The two of them seldom had differences. Dr Singh was respectful to his father and Bhai Mohan Singh doted on his son.

One summer day in the late 1970s, I.P.S. Grover from Ranbaxy's research and development department had gone to the office wing where the rooms of Bhai Mohan Singh and Dr Singh were located. The whole family was holidaying in the cool environs of Kashmir, except for Bhai Mohan Singh, who was in Delhi. Just then, Dr Singh's secretary received a call: it was Dr Singh from Kashmir and he wanted to speak to his father. On hearing this, Bhai Mohan Singh ran from his office barefoot to take the call, afraid that something may be wrong. Fortunately, that was not the case. Grover could see that Bhai Mohan Singh was a bundle of nerves and his eyes were moist. He had never seen such a display of emotions.

Others too could see the special bond between father and son. Soon after he had joined Ranbaxy in the early-1980s, Windlass was sitting with Dr Singh in his office taking instructions. Just then, Bhai Mohan Singh walked in. He was going abroad and had come to see his son. He put his hand on Dr Singh's head, took out Rs 500 from his wallet and pressed the money into his son's hand. The amount was small, but the gesture was heartwarming. Though Dr Singh was a big man by now, his father still treated him like a small child.

As late as in 1990, Prem Bhatia, then editor-in-chief of the *Tribune* and a close friend of Bhai Mohan Singh, wrote: 'Bhai Mohan Singh's happy family life has been one of the main assets which have made his three score years and ten not only eventful and rewarding but which also helped him to live up to the definition of "goodness" as understood by me.'

Dr Singh too respected his parents. Being the first child of his parents, he was closer to his mother. Whenever he was in Delhi, he would meet her every morning—a habit he kept till his last days. He gave both his sons the middle name Mohan—Malvinder Mohan Singh and Shivinder Mohan Singh. The two boys would meet their grandparents every morning before leaving for school to take their blessings. Since Dr Singh was strict and would not let them eat chocolates very often, Bhai Mohan Singh would give them sweets during these early morning meetings on the condition that they did not tell their parents. Every Saturday, Avtar Kaur would lay an elaborate table at lunch for all her grandchildren, pampering each with his or her favourite preparation.

*

Soon after the three brothers split in 1989, Ranbaxy's profitability went up substantially. While the turnover more than doubled from Rs 199.11 crore in 1989-90 to Rs 460.67 crore in 1992-93, the profit after tax shot up from Rs 8.09 crore to Rs 35.34 crore during the period. The company's net worth too increased from Rs 40.64 crore in 1989-90 to Rs 124.56 crore in 1992-93.

At the same time, Manjit's Montari Industries was turning into a financial mess. Analjit's Max India, though profitable, was still small. It had received a blow when Ranbaxy decided to make its own 7ADCA in the early-1990s. Analjit's other venture into BOPP films was close to shutting down. Though Analjit had accepted the division as his destiny, faint murmurs to the effect that the division of assets between the brothers was 'fixed' could now be heard. Manjit alleged that Ranbaxy's financial numbers were deliberately suppressed at the time of the division in order to get himself and Analjit out of Ranbaxy. This was the time when Manjit first levelled the charge that Analjit and he were shortchanged by at least Rs 20 crore each. 'I would rather have a smaller company with a share for all in the family,' Bhai Mohan Singh one day told the management guru Mrityunjay Athreya, while reflecting on the rapid progress made by Ranbaxy in the mid-1990s.

Ranbaxy was now being completely run by professionals. The only members of the family in the new-look executive committee were Bhai Mohan Singh and Dr Singh. Brar had been promoted as president (pharmaceuticals) in 1991, the second-most important position in the company. It was now clear to one and all that Brar was one day going to head the company. Dr Singh trusted his genius totally and would consult him while taking all decisions.

While dividing the assets between his sons, Bhai Mohan Singh had transferred all his Ranbaxy shares to Dr Singh. There was an agreement in the family settlement that Bhai Mohan Singh would be involved in important matters and the company would take care of his expenses on things like housing, medical treatment and travel. Dr Singh's deep attachment and respect for his father gave Bhai Mohan Singh no reason to believe that the transfer of shares could one day result in he being stripped of all powers.

Ranbaxy was more than just an enterprise for Bhai Mohan Singh. To his close friends like Srichand Chhabra, the mercurial chief of the New Delhi Municipal Corporation in the early 1970s, he always referred to the company as his fourth son. He had always been firmly in the saddle. As late as in 1989, when the Bausch & Lomb deal was being negotiated, it was Bhai Mohan Singh who was talking on behalf of Ranbaxy. The sons were nowhere in the picture in the early stages. It was only when Dr Singh expressed his reluctance to go ahead with the venture and Manjit decided to grab the opportunity that the negotiators from Bausch & Lomb got to meet other family members.

The fact that his wings had been clipped soon started preying on Bhai Mohan Singh's mind. And he blamed Dr Singh for it. Life had come a full circle for father and son. From being inseparable, they now got into a bitter struggle for power. It started as a boardroom battle. But once the news broke out, Bhai Mohan Singh was not averse to washing dirty linen in public. Soon, he started telling his friends that Dr Singh was violating the family agreement that Bhai Mohan Singh had the right to veto on any matter that was not to his liking. He also complained that Dr Singh was showing no signs of fulfilling his promise of setting up a trust to enable Bhai Mohan Singh to carry out his charitable activities. Throughout his life, Bhai Mohan Singh had been a generous donor to social and religious causes but now he no longer controlled the purse strings. For the first time in his life, he had to turn back people who sought his financial help. This bruised his ego very badly.

The charge that the separation was fixed did not hold much ground. The valuation of the family's assets was not done by Bhai Mohan Singh or Dr Singh. It was carried out by professionals; Bansi Mehta, the renowned Mumbai-based chartered accountant, had been engaged for this purpose. It was done in a completely transparent manner. Besides, if Ranbaxy numbers had been deliberately suppressed, it is unlikely that the fact would have gone unnoticed by the other brothers, especially Manjit. Though both the brothers were on the executive committee, Manjit was also the company's commercial director with an insider's view of the company's finances.

Dr Singh's friends maintained that the allegations that he had doctored the figures were ridiculous, considering he maintained the highest ethical standards at work. He had been brought up with a very strong sense of values which was reinforced when he became a member of the Radhasoami Satsang.

What had happened was that right through the 1980s, the government exercised a strict price control on drugs and this restricted the profitability of all pharmaceutical companies, including Ranbaxy. In the mid-1980s, when the rupee started falling against the dollar, things took a turn for the worse for companies like Ranbaxy, which still imported the raw material for a host of its products. The company's profitability was getting eroded.

Around the time the brothers split in 1989, the business environment started improving due to several factors. After the severe drought of 1987, a good monsoon in 1988 perked up the economy, which led to an improvement in the liquidity in the markets. Besides, there was a progressive implementation of the Drug Price Control Order, 1987, which removed price controls on several drugs, thus enabling companies like Ranbaxy to raise their prices and, in the process, shore up their bottom line.

Moreover, the launch of Revital and Cifran in 1989 proved extremely successful, with both logging a turnover of Rs 10 crore each within the first year of launch. Soon afterwards, Ranbaxy clinched the cefaclor deal with Eli Lilly. This was really the turning point for the company. Money was flowing into its coffers like never before. Dr Singh could hardly be blamed for the timing of the upturn in business.

That professionals had come to occupy the centrestage is also unlikely to have provoked Bhai Mohan Singh. After all, he had given Dr Singh a free hand when the first wave of professionals were recruited in the early 1970s. Besides, there were well-entrenched professionals in Montari as well as in Max India. If Bhai Mohan Singh's ire was against professionals, he would also have objected to the growing stature of Windlass within Max India. He had come to be called the D.S. Brar of Max India. But he chose not to do so.

The differences between Bhai Mohan Singh and Dr Singh ran deeper. It was a clash between two ways of doing business—the master of the licence-permit-quota raj came into confrontation with the votary of a new, global vision.

*

Bhai Mohan never missed a chance to make friends. 'Everybody was Bhai Mohan Singh's friend and Bhai Mohan Singh was everybody's friend,' Analjit would recall of his father. From bureaucrats to financiers and social activists, Bhai Mohan Singh had time for everyone. He never missed a chance to help his friends. It was a lesson Bhai Mohan Singh had learnt very early in life.

'Do not be angry. Don't quarrel even if you are unhappy. Never shout at others,' Bhai Gyan Chand would often tell his adolescent son. When Bhai Mohan Singh refused to reply to a stranger who greeted him, Bhai Gyan Chand would admonish him, saying he would have got the stranger's blessings if he had replied. Though he had brought up his son as a Sikh, Bhai Gyan Chand would take him to Hindu temples and taught him not to be a religious bigot. The message was driven home quite well—never miss the opportunity to get into the good books of people.

Once Bhai Mohan Singh had joined his father's construction business, he saw another facet of his father's pleasant manners and benevolent disposition. Bhai Gyan Chand had donated Rs 1,50,000 for the construction of a swimming pool for British army officers. The family firm had also put up a refreshments stall at Rawalpindi railway station during the Second World War to cater to soldiers passing through the station. Soon, army officers at Rawalpindi would head straight for Bhai Gyan Chand's house whenever they needed to be bailed out of a tight spot. This was the time that the family had started bidding for army contracts as the government was spending large sums of money on construction during the war years.

Bhai Mohan Singh's father-in-law, Bakshi Dalip Singh, was an equally influential man. Thanks to him, Bhai Mohan Singh had come to be associated with the tuberculosis sanatorium at the picturesque hill station of Murree (now in Pakistan). As a result, Bhai Mohan Singh could get surplus petrol in those days of rationing to drive his family to Murree very frequently. Thanks to his rising reputation with the army officers and the civil administration, Bhai Mohan Singh was even made an honorary magistrate at Rawalpindi.

Once he had shifted to New Delhi, Bhai Mohan Singh was again quick to make friends. Within no time, he became very close to some of the senior bureaucrats of that time like Abid Hussain, who later became the Indian ambassador to the United States, and Naqi Billgrami, a senior Indian Foreign Service (IFS) officer.

When the first government of Delhi was formed under Chaudhary Brahm Prakash, Bhai Mohan Singh was invited to join the New Delhi Municipal Corporation. He continued to serve the corporation for many years. Finally, in 1971, the government awarded him the Padma Shri in recognition of his services. This brought Bhai Mohan Singh in close contact with senior political leaders, and none less than the then President of India, V.V. Giri, inaugurated Ranbaxy's Mohali factory in 1974. It stunned the business world since the factory involved an investment of only Rs 1 crore. The foundation stone of this plant had been laid by the then chief minister of Punjab, Giani Zail Singh, who went on to become the President of India in the 1980s. In November

Ranbaxy's first plant at Mohali being inaugurated by the President of India, V.V. Giri. Also in the picture are Bhai Mohan Singh, Bhai Manjit Singh holding his daughter Niyamat and Dr Singh at the far end.

1978, the chloroquine plant at Mohali was inaugurated by Sardar Prakash Singh Badal, the chief minister of Punjab, and the function was presided over by Jaisukhlal Hathi, who had become the Governor of the state. In 1981, the company's new plant for the manufacture of bulk doxycycline was inaugurated by the then Union minister for petroleum, chemicals and fertilizers, P.C. Sethi and in 1983, the chief minister of Madhya Pradesh, Arjun Singh, laid the foundation stone of the company's new pharmaceutical formulations plant at Dewas.

Once his pharmaceutical business was in full swing, Bhai Mohan Singh became active in the field of public health. He first started working with the Tuberculosis Association of India. Every year, the association kicks off its campaign with the blessings of the President of India. As Bhai Mohan Singh was always a key functionary of the association, this guaranteed him at least one audience with the President every year. By the time he was ready to launch imported diazepam in the country, he had built enough contacts to safeguard himself against any legal problems Roche might raise. In fact, he had taken the government into confidence on the issue. At that time, the Union health minister was Rajkumari Amrit Kaur, who used to refer to Bhai Mohan Singh as 'son'. Bhai Mohan Singh had floated an organization called the All India Society for Prevention of Blindness. While Rajkumari Amrit Kaur was its president, Bhai Mohan Singh was the vice-president and general secretary. She had assured him that he would receive all possible help from the government should Roche decide to create trouble.

A booklet published in January 1974 lists no less than thirty social and religious associations with Bhai Mohan Singh as a key functionary. He was a member of the health ministry's Drugs Technical Advisory Committee for twelve years. When he retired from the committee, Dr Singh stepped in to fill the slot. Thus, the family had a presence on this all-important committee for eighteen years without a break. When Bhai Mohan Singh was elected president of the Indian Drug Manufacturers' Association in 1974, Inder Kumar Gujral, the then information and broadcasting minister, sent a letter calling him a friend. Those were the days when industrialists were viewed with suspicion and politicians did their best to dissociate from them. Gujral and Bhai Mohan Singh had grown up together at Jhelum.

Government patronage was the key to a successful business in those days. Nobody knew this better than Bhai Mohan Singh. Pleasing the political masters of the day was central to business planning. The company's 1971 annual report had, on its first page, a photograph of Bhai Mohan Singh presenting a box of Ranbaxy medicines for the National Relief Fund to Prime Minister Indira Gandhi. The picture shows the prime minister flashing a benevolent smile, a slightly bent Bhai Mohan Singh standing next to her, his hands folded, while P.C. Sethi looks on. The message was clear to all who saw the annual report: Bhai Mohan Singh had access to the Prime Minister's Office. The picture made a reappearance on the first page of the company's 1973 annual report as well.

Bhai Mohan Singh also made several top bureaucrats of the country members of the board. Businessmen always found ex-officials handy during the licence-permit-quota raj when enormous powers of decision-making were vested in the hands of the bureaucrat. Thus, B.P. Patel, a bureaucrat from the elite Indian Civil Services, was brought on the Ranbaxy board as an additional director in October 1974. Patel had served as Secretary in the Union ministry of health and family planning, the managing director of the State Trading Corporation, the government body responsible for 'canalizing' all pharmaceutical imports, and the chairman and managing director of the State Bank of India, the country's largest bank. Three years later, in 1977, another retired bureaucrat, Narottam Sahgal, joined the Ranbaxy board.

*

Dr Singh, in contrast, was hardly a public relations man. He was more comfortable dealing with scientists than with bureaucrats. Unlike Bhai Mohan Singh, who loved to throw parties and entertain the high and mighty at his residence, Dr Singh would seldom call power brokers home. When it became absolutely necessary, he would organize a party at the Ranbaxy guest house at Sunder Nagar.

However, there was often speculation that he was extremely close to Rajiv Gandhi and exercised considerable influence over the young and energetic prime minister.

Dr Singh and Rajiv had met courtesy Vivek Bharat Ram, who was in the same class as Indira Gandhi's elder son in Doon School. Before Rajiv became the prime minister in 1984, the two would meet often at parties at Vivek Bharat Ram's house. They took an instant liking to each other as both of them were forward-looking and wanted India to take rapid strides in science and technology. Even after becoming prime minister, Rajiv would always take time out for Dr Singh.

However, Dr Singh did not know Rajiv well enough to curry favours with him. Still, Dr Singh was grief-stricken when Raizada informed him of Rajiv's assassination in 1991. He was in the United States when he was given the news, and he broke down on the phone.

*

By the late-1980s, before anybody else in India, Dr Singh knew that things were going to change in the pharmaceutical business. The protection offered by the patent regime would have to go as India integrated with the global economy. He was aware of the drift of the patent negotiations at the multilateral trade negotiations, the precursor to the World Trade Organization (WTO) and knew that the days of unprotected product patents were numbered.

His close associates like Bimal Raizada first got to know

of his changed views around 1988, when he ordered that Ranbaxy stop funding the National Council for Patent Laws, a voluntary organization managed by one B.K. Keyala, which was arguing that India did not require patents of any kind. Keyala was funded by both Ranbaxy and Cipla. Once Dr Singh realized that Keyala was fighting a lost cause, he pulled out. Cipla, however, continued to fund Keyala for many more years. Cipla's Hamied was always bitterly opposed to any change in the patent laws, arguing passionately against India's commitment to reintroduce product patents from 1 January 2005.

Though he had started discussing the matter with friends and colleagues, it was only in his management review for 1993-94 that Dr Singh first made public his changed views on the subject:

> For the Indian pharmaceutical industry, the GATT (General Agreement on Tariff and Trade) treaty signalled the emergence of a new era with the acceptance of product patents. Although some in the industry have misgivings on the issue, we at Ranbaxy believe that this can provide new opportunities. With the new Intellectual Property Rights regime that India has agreed upon, focus must now shift to innovation. Industry has not been investing adequately on research and development, as profit margins have remained low on account of a rigid price control mechanism. The future belongs to those companies who will invest and enhance their research capabilities, initiate change and avail themselves of the emerging opportunities.

This meant that Ranbaxy had to alter its style of functioning. To begin with, the top decision-making body of the company had to have the best brains within Ranbaxy. After the 1989 split, Dr Singh got the opportunity to restructure the executive committee. While the earlier twelve-member committee had five family members—Bhai Mohan Singh, his three sons and Jaswant Singh—and one diehard loyalist in Sawhney, the new committee of six had only two family members, Bhai Mohan Singh and Dr Singh, while the other four—Sheth, Raizada, Brar and Chakroborty—were professionals. The next year, Jag Mohan Khanna was co-opted into this high-powered body.

The next imperative was that Ranbaxy had to take risks in research and development. Money would have to be pumped into research to develop new products with no guarantee that the investment would one day pay off. Dr Singh was convinced that for Ranbaxy to do well abroad, it had to first consolidate its position at home. Ranbaxy was not even present in all segments of the Indian market. It was largely an anti-infectives company and it needed to expand its product portfolio in double quick time. This could be done only through acquisitions and mergers, which called for a total change in mindset. An all-stock acquisition deal or a merger could dilute the family's stake in Ranbaxy. Also, all the expansion plans drawn up by Dr Singh required fresh infusion of capital into the company. This, again, would have called for a dilution in the promoter's stake in the company. All this was too radical for Bhai Mohan Singh.

*

Bhai Mohan Singh had little contribution to make to the new Ranbaxy. The P.V. Narasimha Rao government had opened up the Indian economy in 1991, sounding the death knell of the licence-permit-quota raj. The skills of environment management, which Bhai Mohan Singh had honed to perfection, were rendered redundant overnight. In a break from the past, management discussion would now focus on global pharmaceutical trends. Bhai Mohan Singh felt alienated.

Dr Singh was only too aware of his father's dilemma. But he still had a role cut out for him. He wanted Bhai Mohan Singh to be Ranbaxy's face at business forums and industry associations. But this alone was unacceptable to Bhai Mohan Singh.

The differences slowly started appearing during board meetings. Dr Singh could sense resistance from Bhai Mohan Singh and some of his friends on the company's board. He knew he was running a race against time, and it was only natural for him to feel frustrated. Initially, it appeared that Dr Singh was going to lose the boardroom battle.

One day he called his friends from the executive committee and told them that it was soon going to be all over. He offered to give them some financial compensation out of his own pocket, once he was ousted from the board. These top professionals of the Indian pharmaceutical industry threw in their lot with Dr Singh. They gave him undated resignation letters to be used as the final gambit if he was cornered. Though the father and son were fighting inside the boardroom, it had not affected the company at all as the day-to-day running of the company was entrusted to professionals. If these people were to pull out of the company, Ranbaxy would come to a grinding halt.

Others in the company too had come out in support of Dr Singh. During a board meeting at Ranbaxy's office in the Nehru Place commercial complex in south Delhi, some fifty executives marched to the boardroom, shouting slogans in favour of Dr Singh. They were led by Sanjiv Kaul, who had started his innings at Ranbaxy in 1983, when he joined the company's international division. (He later went on to become in-charge of Ranbaxy's operations in China, the head of the India region and then the head of corporate affairs.) When he opened the door of the boardroom, he paused to look back at his other colleagues. There was no one there. Kaul's heart sank. Yet, he said his bit and walked back. Soon, some of the directors were baying for his blood but Dr Singh's intervention saved the day for him.

The fight started turning in Dr Singh's favour when Prof. Veda Vyas, Rustom P. Soonawala, Narottam Sahgal and D.D. Chopra resigned from the company's board of directors, effective from 18 September 1992. In their place, Dr Singh was quick to appoint Mumbai-based businessman Tirath R. Mulchandani, Vivek Bharat Ram, Vikram Lal of the Eicher group and the journalist Suman Dubey; all of them were his friends. (By now, Vivek Bharat Ram and Dr Singh had grown very close to each other.) They would speak to each other every day. In a move that would strengthen Dr Singh's position further on the board, Brar and Sheth were appointed as alternate directors between September 1992 and November 1992. Dubey, however, resigned soon after joining when he became in-charge of Dow Jones, the financial news agency, in India. The boardroom strengths of the two warring factions were now evenly matched.

Soon, sparks began to fly. Dr Singh rarely uttered a word against his father, but his friends did not hold their punches. They targeted Bhai Mohan Singh's friends on the board. Though professionals were invited to join the Ranbaxy board even as early as in the 1960s, Bhai Mohan Singh was not averse to packing the board with relatives and friends; Avtar Kaur served on the Ranbaxy board till 1983. When the fight with his son erupted, there were three board members, apart from Manjit, who decided to side with Bhai Mohan Singh: Dan Singh Bawa, Air Marshal O.P. Mehra and M.M. Sabharwal.

Bawa, a Delhi-based businessman with interests in construction and real estate, had joined Ranbaxy after Lepetit exited from the company. Air Marshal Mehra had studied with Bhai Mohan Singh in Government College, Lahore, and joined the Ranbaxy board in 1987. There was a tacit understanding that if he did not agree with Bhai Mohan Singh on any resolution that the latter was seeking to pass at the board meetings, Mehra would abstain from voting.

Sabharwal had first met Bhai Mohan Singh in 1980 as they were both members of the PHDCCI (Punjab, Haryana and Delhi Chambers of Commerce and Industry). Sabharwal's first impression was that Bhai Mohan Singh was an extremely cordial man with excellent contacts in government as well as diplomatic circles. It was clear to Sabharwal that, in a very pleasant way, Bhai Mohan Singh wielded a lot of influence in the corridors of power and that the mild-mannered Sikh had used the licence raj to ensure Ranbaxy's growth. In 1984, Bhai Mohan Singh invited Sabharwal, who had by then earned a reputation as a fine corporate director, to join the Ranbaxy board. If Sabharwal had a high opinion of Bhai Mohan Singh and how he had developed the craft of 'environment management' to perfection, the Ranbaxy chairman too had every reason to be impressed with the tall and elegant technocrat.

After graduating from Delhi's St. Stephen's College in 1942, Sabharwal chanced upon a job advertisement put out by Dunlop, the tyre company, for management trainees on a salary of Rs 75 per month, and decided to apply. However, the British employment manager there tried his best to dissuade Sabharwal from joining. He relented only when he learnt that Sabharwal's father had been awarded the Order of the British Empire (OBE). Little did the employment manager know that he was interviewing the future executive chairman of Dunlop and that in 1998, Sabharwal too would receive an OBE for his role in promoting Indo-British partnership in social welfare.

Sabharwal retired as the executive chairman of Dunlop in 1977. Soon afterwards, he was co-opted into the board of several multinational companies in India like Bata India, Britannia Industries, Indian Oxygen and a few public sector undertakings like Oil India and the National Aluminium Company. In the early and mid-1980s, Sabharwal was to once again earn a name for himself as the non-executive chairman of Britannia as well as Bata.

During a Britannia board meeting in 1981, he found that the company's opening stock for a month did not tally with the previous month's closing stock. Inquiries revealed that all was not well with the company's finances and Sabharwal realized that the only way out was to remove the managing director, the finance director and the marketing director of the company. He got permission from the principal shareholder of Britannia at that time—the United Kingdom-based Huntley and Palmer Foods. On consulting some lawyers, Sabharwal realized that secrecy was of utmost importance in such an operation. He went about the task in a manner that verged on the Machiavellian, and managed a smooth purge.

A few years later, Sabharwal once again played a stellar role in defusing a crisis, this time as the non-executive chairman of Bata. The shoe company had imported some raw material and exported footwear made from it, against which it got a refund of the import duty it paid. One day, a Bata India employee informed the government that the company was claiming duty drawbacks on exports that did not use imported raw material at all. The law enforcement agencies immediately raided the company's offices and factories all over the country. The managing director of the company was taken into custody. This was the time when V.P. Singh (who was to become prime minister in 1989) was the finance minister in Rajiv Gandhi's government and was cracking down on economic offences by corporate bodies.

Sabharwal called a meeting of the Bata board in Kolkata to discuss the whole issue. At the meeting, he offered to help the company in getting out of the jam, provided the board passed a resolution giving him the sole authority to handle the crisis. With no other solution in sight, the board had no option but to agree. Back in Delhi, Sabharwal sought a meeting with the Cabinet Secretary, P.K. Kaul. After their meeting, Kaul called up Vinod Pande, the Finance Secretary, asking him to see Sabharwal. Pande told Sabharwal bluntly that the only way out for the company was to accept that it had violated the law, tender an apology and give back to the government the excess duty drawbacks it had got.

It was not an easy choice for Sabharwal. The admission of wrongdoing by Bata could be used against the company in the future. There was not enough time to call the Bata headquarters in Canada for advice. Not knowing what to do, he telephoned Kaul who also asked him to submit an apology. Sabharwal sent an apology on behalf of Bata and, later in the day, was informed by Pande that the government had decided to drop the investigations but would give publicity to this case.

The next morning, Sabharwal got a telephone call from John Elliott, the local *Financial Times* representative, who told him that the government had announced Bata's apology at a press conference and asked Sabharwal if he would like to comment. Sabharwal had to decide quickly. This particular report had the potential to damage Bata's reputation globally. He gave a simple statement: 'If we make a mistake at Bata, we set it right immediately.' The Bata image was saved. Thomas Bata himself acknowledged Sabharwal's efforts in handling this crisis.

When Sabharwal joined the Ranbaxy board in 1984, there was no tacit understanding with Bhai Mohan Singh that Sabharwal would toe his line. Though the two of them were fairly well acquainted, Bhai Mohan Singh did not know Sabharwal well enough to extract such a commitment from him. Sabharwal had Dr Singh's respect too and the latter would often consult him on important matters. So why did Sabharwal side with Bhai Mohan Singh in the fight? Sabharwal felt that while Dr Singh was a man in a hurry, Bhai Mohan Singh was more conservative and wanted to ensure that the plans for rapid growth should not end in disaster. After all, Sabharwal had been witness to what had happened at Dunlop. The company had borrowed heavily to bankroll its ambitious expansion plans. Once the projected cash generation did not take place, Dunlop got mired in a financial crisis. He was apprehensive that Dr Singh's ambitious plans could similarly spell doom for Ranbaxy.

Still, Bhai Mohan Singh's supporters could feel the tide turning against them. As recounted by several board members present there, tempers ran so high that at one particular meeting, Capt. Amarinder Singh, who had studied with Dr Singh and who had joined the Ranbaxy board in 1983, told Bhai Mohan Singh that he would physically pick him up and remove him from the boardroom. Capt. Singh, who belonged to the former royal family of Patiala and later became the chief minister of Punjab, would not attend Ranbaxy board meetings regularly on account of his political engagements. Yet he strode into this board meeting to make a point in his own very emphatic style. Having made his statement, he snapped a pencil into two. The message was not lost on those present.

*

By now, Bhai Mohan Singh and Dr Singh were no longer on talking terms. Dr Singh would go to meet his mother every day, but Bhai Mohan Singh refused to see him. The fight took its heaviest toll on Avtar Kaur. She was torn between her husband and her favourite son. This was the time her health started failing and she never regained her energy. She died in July 2004 after a prolonged illness. But Dr Singh continued to meet her till he could stand on his feet. During his last days, when he knew his time was up, Dr Singh assured his mother that after him, Malvinder would look after her and she would not feel his absence.

Several friends of Bhai Mohan Singh as well as Dr Singh tried to resolve the crisis but in vain. Sabharwal and Avtar

Kaur went several times to counsel Dr Singh when father and son were not on talking terms. But he refused to relent. Bansi Mehta also tried to bring them together. But relations between the two had soured to such an extent that Bhai Mohan Singh wrote a letter to Dr Singh saying that there was no need for him to attend his funeral. Athreya's bid to help patch things up too met with no success. 'It is not easy to get Punjabis to compromise,' he would remember years later.

Air Marshal Mehra too tried to broker peace between father and son. A decade after the spat, sitting on the lawns of his home in New Delhi, he would recount how all his efforts were gently blocked by Dr Singh. 'He told me that he appreciated my concern, but this was a matter between him and his father. The words were chosen very carefully. He didn't say it was a matter between him and the chairman of the company. I got the message and did not pursue the matter any further,' he said.

Perhaps the most sincere efforts to bring the warring father and son together were made by Prem Pandhi, an old friend of Bhai Mohan Singh, from their college days. Pandhi went on to become the executive chairman of Cadbury India. Bhai Mohan Singh had offered him a berth on the Montari board. Pandhi told Bhai Mohan Singh several times to let things go. But his old friend would not listen. 'He was extremely worked up and was boiling from inside,' Pandhi was to recall. He even tried to reason with Dr Singh by telling him that all that his father wanted was some importance and not to snatch the business from him. But their efforts came to naught.

It was more than a personality clash for Dr Singh. He had to win against his father if Ranbaxy had to be put on the path to high growth. The ambitious plans he had drawn for the company would all be scrapped if he lost the battle. Ranbaxy would have remained an India-focussed company. He couldn't let it happen.

On 6 February 1993, Bhai Mohan Singh, Air Marshal Mehra, Sabharwal, Bawa and Manjit resigned from the Ranbaxy board of directors. The same day, Dr Singh took over as the chairman and managing director of the company. Bhai Mohan Singh was made chairman emeritus. The previous night, Manjit had come to know that there were plans to oust Bhai Mohan Singh in the board meeting scheduled for the day. He disclosed this to his father. Rather than be ousted unceremoniously, Bhai Mohan Singh chose to resign. Along with him, his friends also resigned. The boardroom battle was over, though the fight between father and son would continue.

*

Bhai Mohan Singh now took the fight to the courts, charging Dr Singh with reneging on the commitments made in the family settlement to give money for his charities. When Dr Singh died in 1999, Malvinder and Shivinder got embroiled in the legal cases. Even when Dr Singh was diagnosed with cancer, there was no thaw in relations. Though Bhai Mohan Singh did visit his son while he was undergoing treatment at the Sloane-Kettering hospital in the United States, the meetings were frosty and the uneasiness between the two was not lost on all who were present. It was not a meeting of father and son in the traditional Indian way. 'The normal empathy for a son dying so young was not there,' Dr P.S. Joshi, director of the Radhasoami Hospital at Beas, who was present during these meetings, would remember later.

But the fight did upset Dr Singh. In his last interview to the media, about a month before his death, he mentioned the ugly spat with his father as the only regret he had. He would invariably tell his close friends how going against his father had hurt him.

Once Dr Singh died, Bhai Mohan Singh made one last

attempt to regain control of the company. Though he did not make any formal demand, he told the media that the promoter family should be represented on the Ranbaxy board and, therefore, Malvinder and Shivinder, should be inducted on the board right away. But Dr Singh had made it very clear that his sons would join the board only on their merit, when they had developed enough skills and knowledge to add value to all boardroom discussions. The conviction was as strong as ever during his final interview a month before he died. Though his body was frail, his eyes shone like those of a determined warrior. There was no mistaking that not even death could shake his belief. Both the sons were in their mid-twenties and did not have much work experience at the time of their father's death. They understood that whatever Dr Singh had willed was in the best interests of the company. Once Bhai Mohan Singh started voicing his

Bhai Mohan Singh meets former President Bill Clinton in October 2002 when Ranbaxy held its board meeting in the US. Bhai Mohan Singh had been specially flown in to address the meeting.

demand, they promptly issued a statement saying that they would abide by their father's philosophy of separating ownership of an enterprise from its management. That put paid to Bhai Mohan Singh's last efforts to get the family back on the driving seat.

*

Brar had become the symbol of executive power during the fight. Bhai Mohan Singh had directed much of his ire against him. Over the years, once Brar started delivering the results, Bhai Mohan Singh mellowed down. He would send him congratulatory letters, seeking his advice on various matters regularly. And Brar reciprocated the gesture. In 2002, when Ranbaxy decided to hold a board meeting in New Jersey, Bhai Mohan Singh too attended it as the company's chairman emeritus. Overwhelmed by the reception he got and the results turned in by the company his son had built, Bhai Mohan Singh broke down. He lavished praises on his son like never before.

In 2003, after it was announced that Ranbaxy had been chosen the company of the year by the *Economic Times*, Bhai Mohan Singh sent a cheque of Rs 50,000 to Brar to organize a tea for the company's senior executives. Brar sent the cheque back, assuring Bhai Mohan Singh that a tea would be held but at the company's expense. Finally, everything was all right again.

8

Stepping on to the World Stage

By 2002, a substantial part of the turnover of a large number of Indian companies was coming from their overseas business. Ranbaxy, too, was getting more business from abroad than from India. The United States had emerged as its largest market accounting for 39 per cent of its total sales. While planning for the future, Ranbaxy had started projecting 50 per cent business coming from the United States, 25 per cent from Europe, 12 per cent from India and the rest from other markets of the world. As the United States accounted for almost half the world market for pharmaceutical products, Ranbaxy's alignment with the global markets would require it to derive an equal proportion of its sales from this market.

By the early-1980s, Ranbaxy had arrived at the conclusion that it could not grow by restricting itself to the domestic market. Besides, with the government controlling drug prices, profits could not grow beyond a point. Prices in the unregulated market were far better; any drug would sell in west Asia at prices four to six times higher than in

India. It was, therefore, decided that the company would derive at least half of its turnover from exports. With this in view, a separate international department was set up under Brar in 1983.

*

Dr Singh immediately after he became the chairman and managing director of Ranbaxy.

Actually, Ranbaxy's overseas business had started soon after it launched Calmpose. In January 1969, it hired Ravinder Kumar Manchanda to develop its export markets. Manchanda had been working in a Danish company, East Asiatic, which had wound up its operations in India. When he joined Ranbaxy, it didn't take him long to realize that the company was not very serious about exports and was only trying to avail of export incentives. Besides, Ranbaxy was still a very small company and a marginal player in the domestic market. Therefore, for it to think of exports was ridiculous.

Ranbaxy realized that, like India, there were other developing countries that did not recognize product patents. Drug prices in these countries were high because local production of medicines was very limited and the markets were dominated by global pharmaceutical companies. When India went off the product patent regime, Ranbaxy was amongst the first Indian companies to develop reverse engineering skills and it set up a bulk drug facility so that these skills could translate into commercially viable processes. It could, therefore, produce drugs that were under patent in the developed markets at a fraction of the cost and it could make a killing if these drugs could be exported to the developing country markets.

With this in mind, Dr Singh and Manchanda embarked on a whirlwind tour of Hong Kong, Singapore, Indonesia, Thailand and Malaysia in 1970. The company executed its first export order to Mauritius that year and soon after started exporting to other developing markets as well. Though the volumes were low, profits were handsome. The company, therefore, decided to press ahead with its export plans, though patent-holding companies tried every trick they could to trip Ranbaxy up.

The first threat of legal action came in the mid-1970s from ICI, the then diversified United Kingdom-based conglomerate. Ranbaxy had exported some quantities of chlorfibrate to Malaysia against a government tender, an action that prompted ICI to issue a legal notice. The six-page telegram that landed at Ranbaxy's Okhla office said that the company could not export the drug as ICI held the patent. After consulting its lawyers, Ranbaxy countered that there was no patent infringement whatsoever as the drug was being produced in India, which did not recognize product patents, and sold in Malaysia, which too did not recognize such patents. ICI should, it further said, take the matter up with the Malaysian government, which was importing the medicine from Ranbaxy. The matter ended there.

ICI had a virtual monopoly in the chlorfibrate market in Malaysia. Realizing that this monopoly position would be threatened once Ranbaxy was able to establish a foothold in the market with its cheaper drug, it tried to scare away what it saw as a small and unknown Indian company, using a hectoring tone. However, Ranbaxy had done its homework well and showed more courage than ICI anticipated. As ICI feared, Ranbaxy broke its fifteen-year monopoly of the chlorfibrate market in Malaysia.

Soon, Ranbaxy was under attack from several multinational pharmaceutical companies—Roche objected to its exports of diazepam to Singapore, while Winthrop raised a hue and cry over exports of Fortwin to Sri Lanka. But they couldn't stop Ranbaxy. Nor could Glaxo do anything when the two companies clashed in the United Arab Emirates (UAE) market.

Ranbaxy had identified the UAE as a lucrative market. It was a rich country and the drug prices there were quite steep. The UAE government would import drugs only from American and European drug companies. However, the kingdom did not recognize product patents. Moreover, there were a large number of Indian doctors in the UAE, who could be persuaded to prescribe medicines manufactured by an Indian company, especially to expatriate Indians. Soon, Ranbaxy was selling its products in the UAE.

One of the drugs that Ranbaxy had done reverse engineering on was ranitidine, an anti-ulcer drug which Glaxo had launched in 1981 under the brand Zantac. It had become the world's top-selling medicine by 1986 and had catapulted Glaxo amongst the pioneers of medicinal research. Once the drug was well established in the developed markets, Glaxo had started selling it in countries which did not have product patents. It was confident that there would be no threat to its ranitidine monopoly. Till Ranbaxy entered the market, with its ranitidine at a price less than half of Glaxo's. Glaxo was so upset that it did not respond positively when, in the late-1980s, Ranbaxy initiated talks to sell bulk ranitidine as it had excess capacity. It even threatened to sue Ranbaxy in London over its ranitidine exports to the UAE.

Lobbying hard with the UAE government, Glaxo got Ranbaxy's ranitidine de-registered in that country. Apart from raising the issue of patent violation, Glaxo also alleged that a drug being sold so cheap could not be effective. Ranbaxy decided to fight back. It challenged the local administration to have its ranitidine samples, collected from chemist shops and not provided by the company, checked in the best laboratories in the United Kingdom—Glaxo's home country—for efficacy. It also got Indian doctors to lobby with the government in its favour, questioning why they should prescribe an expensive medicine when cheaper alternatives were available. Finally, the UAE government picked up samples of Ranbaxy's ranitidine from the market and sent it to the United Kingdom for testing. The results showed that Ranbaxy's drug was as effective as that of Glaxo. Finally, after a year and a half, the UAE allowed Ranbaxy to sell its ranitidine in the market once again. Glaxo was left with no choice but to drop prices—it cut the ranitidine price tag by half.

*

Ranbaxy was also one of the first Indian pharmaceutical companies to set up factories abroad. In the mid-1970s, it had studied prospects of putting up a plant in four countries: Canada, Ireland, Mauritius and Nigeria. Bhai Mohan Singh himself travelled to Canada, Ireland and Nigeria to get a feel of the market. The initial reports were not very favourable; though all these markets were big, it would be extremely difficult for a foreign company, especially an unknown drug manufacturer from India, to raise bank credit.

Then an opportunity presented itself. Ranbaxy had been exporting to Nigeria since the early 1970s. It was a large country and its pharmaceutical market was unregulated. As there was no local production, Nigeria depended on exports from the United States and drug prices, therefore, were quite high. Ranbaxy had exported a consignment of medicine to Nigeria, which the importer refused to pick up. Dr Singh then called up his close friend, Nigeria-based businessman Jetha Daryani, to help him find another importer. Daryani, who had been toying with the idea of manufacturing medicine in Nigeria, proposed an alliance with Ranbaxy to set up shop in the country. The idea appealed to Dr Singh. In 1977, Ranbaxy started its Nigerian operations by setting up a plant to make liquids as Ranbaxy Montari Nigeria Ltd.

However, the company's representatives could not go to doctors with liquids alone; they needed other pharmaceutical products as well. These were exported from Ranbaxy in India. Even the caps and bottles used for packaging suspensions were sent from India. It was a win-win situation for Ranbaxy. Its officials were reluctant to go to Nigeria because of the poor law and order situation (the Ranbaxy plant got burgled once), but the company offered handsome incentives; children of some key officials were sent to expensive boarding schools in India and England. Though Ranbaxy had only a 10 per cent stake in the venture, it was running the business. As a result, after two years, the company started declaring hefty dividends in excess of 100 per cent.

Nigeria also opened the door to other parts of Africa. Ranbaxy found that drug prices in former French colonies like Cameroon, Senegal and Cote d'Ivoire were extremely high. These countries were extremely poor and were totally dependent on their former rulers for medicines. However, the market was not an easy one to crack. To begin with, the locals did not like to do business in any language except

French. Besides, Ranbaxy had no contacts in these countries.

Ranbaxy befriended a local power broker in Cameroon. An African educated in Paris, he had sixteen wives and had sired a small army of children. Ranbaxy brought him and his sixteenth wife to India for an all-expenses paid holiday. Impressed, he helped Ranbaxy set up a local office in Cameroon, as required by the law. Special labels in French were printed and Ranbaxy hired local medical representatives. Profits on sales were as high as between 200 and 300 per cent. From Cameroon, Ranbaxy spread its wings to Senegal and Cote d'Ivoire.

After some initial profits, the Nigerian joint venture had started totting up losses by the mid-1980s because Ranbaxy did not have full control over the company. The agreement calling for joint decision making between the two partners had taken its toll on the company's bottom line. In 1989, Ranbaxy sold its 10 per cent stake to its local partner and set up its own 100 per cent subsidiary. To ensure a smooth transition for the old company, Ranbaxy leased a handful of its brands to it for three years. The new Ranbaxy unit was profitable from the first year of inception and was soon to become one of the top five pharmaceutical companies in Nigeria.

Meanwhile, in 1982, Ranbaxy decided to set up another overseas joint venture, this time in Malaysia. Though Ranbaxy had been planning to take a controlling 51 per cent stake in the joint venture, the Malaysian government gave permission for only a 49 per cent stake. The final approval came only in late-1985 and the production unit went on stream in July 1987.

In 1984, Ranbaxy formed its third overseas joint venture in Thailand. As Thai law also did not permit an overseas company to take a controlling stake in a local venture, Ranbaxy kept a 49 per cent stake and had to place a large chunk of equity with some Thai businessmen of Indian origin and some doctors. Unichem too had set up a manufacturing unit in Thailand, but had lost interest in the venture. Unichem's man in Thailand had taken over the company and retained the Unichem name. Ranbaxy acquired this unit and later divested it, choosing to either import the products from India or get these manufactured on contract by a third party to meet its specifications in Thailand itself.

Ranbaxy took its operations in Nigeria, Malaysia and Thailand very seriously. Though it faced various issues in each of them, it was in these markets that it learnt the basic principles of international business: high quality, customer focus, on-time delivery and right price.

By 1991-92, the company had come to realize that in order to cater to the fast-growing Chinese market, it would have to set up a unit in that country. At the 1992 annual general meeting, shareholders were told that a joint venture in Hong Kong was on the cards. In what was to be the first Sino-Indian business joint venture, the company had, within the next one year, signed an agreement to set up a joint venture subsidiary at Guangzhou for producing and marketing of formulations. It hoped to operationalize the plant by early-1995. Meanwhile, by 1993-94, Cifran had established itself as one of the leading pharmaceutical brands in China.

*

Before the international department was set up in 1983, Sawhney, the head of marketing, was in charge of exports as well. However, the company found that the overseas market was different, with its own regulatory framework. The function, therefore, needed separate treatment. The name—the international department and not export department—showed that the company had more than just exports in mind. One of the first persons Brar recruited for his team was Sanjiv Kaul.

Immediately after passing out of the Indian Institute of

Management, Ahmedabad, in 1980, Kaul joined Sandoz and moved to Roche three years later. After about a year, Kaul came across a newspaper advertisement put out by Ranbaxy, which was looking for a sales manager for its export business. Kaul had an irresistible urge to respond to the advertisement. He had met Brar briefly while he was passing out of business school, and had been deeply impressed. At that time, he did not respond to Brar's offer because he wanted to start his career with a multinational company. Now he felt Brar calling him through this advertisement. He just knew that the job was made for him. Within no time, he had moved from Mumbai to Delhi to work for Ranbaxy. Years later, Kaul would still speak passionately of his formative years at Ranbaxy: 'If given the chance, I would love to relive those years once again. Ranbaxy is a truly blessed company, driven by a very powerful divine force. We are propelled by a mysterious hand, which gives us the answers when everything seems lost. Something has always bailed us out.'

Kaul quickly found his space in Ranbaxy. When he met Dr Singh, he was convinced that Ranbaxy was an organization that was committed to growth and wanted to chart its own destiny. The company was aggressive and willing to take on any challenge in the marketplace. He had not witnessed this never-ending rush of adrenalin at either Sandoz or Roche.

In 1985, Kaul was sent to Kenya to study the market and come up with a business plan. When he returned, Kaul had drawn up projections which he thought were fairly aggressive: from Rs 5 lakh in the first year to Rs 10 lakh in the second and Rs 20 lakh in the third. Expecting to be praised, Kaul was stunned when his projections were torn apart for being extremely modest. He realized he had been thinking very small. Even though he was being mauled at the meeting, Kaul was enjoying every moment; his mind had been opened up to business possibilities. Kaul was soon back with a new set of projections—from Rs 2 lakh in the first year to Rs 2 crore in the third year.

That same year, Kaul also went to Egypt to assess the market for ampicillin. On realizing that there was a better demand for amoxycillin, he called up Brar from Cairo to apprise him of the situation. He was not sure how Brar would react since at that time, ampicillin was the blockbuster in Ranbaxy's portfolio and the company was not even making amoxycillin. Kaul was not sure if Brar would heed his advice. But not only did Ranbaxy start making the drug shortly, it also started exports to Egypt.

*

In all its export plans, Ranbaxy had consciously decided to stay out of the Union of Soviet Socialist Republics (USSR), though several Indian companies had made their fortunes in trade with that country in the 1980s and up to the early 1990s, when the Soviet bloc collapsed.

As India had run up a huge trade deficit with the USSR largely on account of military supplies, Indian companies were told that they could export to the USSR and get their payments from the Reserve Bank of India in rupees. This suited the USSR very well. Many Indian exporters would often import drugs in large quantities from western countries, including the United States, for exports to the USSR. In other words, India was shelling out foreign exchange for drug imports by the Soviet Union and, later, its splinter republics. The Indian drug companies, for their part, had no reason to complain. They could get substantial export turnover without any efforts at market development.

Senior officials of Medexpo, the agency that would hand out export quotas to Indian companies, would descend in India in droves every year. Indian drug companies went out of their way to please their guests, providing them with whatever they demanded: large sums of cash, the choicest wine and, at times, even women. In return, the officials would hand out supply contracts on their return.

Though Ranbaxy also did some nominal business with Medexpo, the company preferred to stay away from a regulated economy. So while the chiefs of most pharmaceutical companies would camp in Delhi whenever the Medexpo team came visiting, Dr Singh and Brar ignored them and left their juniors to deal with them. A few meetings and a lunch for the visiting delegation was the maximum that Ranbaxy would do. As a result, Ranbaxy remained a fringe player in the Medexpo business.

However, Ranbaxy became the first company to set up shop in Russia after the collapse of the Soviet Union in 1991. Soon after, it had the largest presence amongst Indian pharmaceutical companies in the Commonwealth of Independent States (CIS). By 1994-95, Ranbaxy was well entrenched in both Russia and Ukraine. Since Russia was the core market in the CIS region, the company was quick to establish full-fledged medical services and a regulatory department there.

*

In 1987-88, Ranbaxy took the pioneering step of exporting bulk drugs from India to a regulated market, even though the margins were not high compared to the domestic market where high profits were possible because the bulk drug market was protected. But the company knew that it would have to make such sacrifices in order to propel long-term growth. It thus became the first Indian company to export bulk drugs and laid the foundations for the business model adopted by most other Indian pharmaceutical companies a decade later.

Ranbaxy was the first Indian company to sense this opportunity. It knew that pharmaceutical producers were under pressure throughout the world to reduce the price of generic medicine, forcing them to outsource manufacturing to low-cost producers. Ranbaxy, by now, was one of the largest producers of ampicillin in Asia. This gave it a distinct price advantage over others.

A few years after its first exports of bulk drugs to unregulated markets, Ranbaxy started exports of bulk drugs to Europe. Some European countries allowed companies to test the bulk drugs themselves, as a result of which Ranbaxy did not have to go through lengthy approval processes as in the United States, where the efficacy of drugs is first established by the USFDA. It also got some orders for ampicillin from the United States, but these were for exports to third countries (some of it also found its way back to India) and not for consumption in the United States.

Initially, like most exporters, Ranbaxy did business through some contacts in each country. Brar soon put an end to the practice, arguing that since the agent would have other interests as well, he would not give enough time to develop Ranbaxy's business. Brar said that posting Ranbaxy's own personnel would help the company in the long run. Thus, Ranbaxy staffers were sent to places like Vietnam, Poland, Russia and Thailand to study the market and give their reports. They were told not to worry about generating profits from day one. It was yet another bold move, which soon started paying rich dividends.

By the early-1990s, Ranbaxy had signed the cefaclor deal with Eli Lilly. This took its global business into a different orbit.

*

The cefaclor success gave Dr Singh the financial backing and the confidence in Ranbaxy's research and development capabilities to translate his vision of making Ranbaxy a global company into reality. The first thing he did was to articulate his vision and put in place a mission statement along with a set of values worthy of a global company. Apart from his drive to make Ranbaxy a multinational pharmaceutical company, there was another reason for Dr Singh to push through this exercise. His accession to the Ranbaxy top slot in February 1993 after the bitter boardroom fight with his father had battered Ranbaxy's image and it was up to him to set it right once again.

Though he had discussed his vision with his close colleagues, Dr Singh needed somebody who could give it a final shape and help implement it. Like all forward-looking businessmen of his time, he was aware that he needed to overhaul the organization in order to move ahead. He needed somebody who could act as his sounding board as well as guide him through the reorganization of the business. He got in touch with Mrityunjay Athreya, a management guru who combined deep-rooted Indian values with management theory.

Dr Singh had first met Athreya in 1986 when both of them were nominated to a government committee headed by the industrialist Ratan Tata to look into why several mega-projects announced by the private sector had not taken off. By then, Athreya had emerged as the country's top management consultant, sought after by corporate chieftains as the foremost authority on strategic thinking and modern-age management practices. Soon after the first meeting itself, Dr Singh knew Athreya was the man who could help him chart a new course for Ranbaxy. But he could not engage Athreya's services since he was not in full control of the company. Once he gained control of Ranbaxy, Dr Singh moved fast and brought Athreya on board.

By then, Athreya too had developed a healthy respect for Dr Singh. He admired the latter's dedication towards building a strong Indian pharmaceutical company and respected Dr Singh's confidence in the ability of Indian scientists. 'He had a great fighting spirit and did not like India to have a subordinate status in the world. That India should be dependent on multinationals for healthcare was totally unacceptable to him. He wanted to marry science and business. My job was to give a total management model for it,' Athreya would later say.

His interface with Dr Singh convinced him that Ranbaxy had what it would take to become another Teva, which had, by the early-1990s, emerged not only as the largest pharmaceutical company in Israel but also as a leading player in the world generics market. Teva was founded in Jerusalem in 1901 as a small wholesale drug business that distributed imported medicines, which were loaded onto the backs of camels and donkeys, to customers throughout the land. In the 1930s, a number of Jewish scientists and chemists emigrated from Europe to Palestine and they began building medical and pharmaceutical businesses. Among them were Teva, Zori and Assia, all three of which were to come together in the 1970s. Over the years, Teva showed a phenomenal growth in the generics business, while kicking off its own programme for new drugs.

When he first visited the Ranbaxy offices and met key functionaries, Athreya found that though the company was bristling with raw energy and had a strong sales team, its managerial skills required work. The challenges in various functions were not sufficiently high. Finance, for instance, was more about accounting than about planning the company's growth. Far from working in tandem as a team, the people making bulk drugs and those making formulations were competing with each other. In short, there was a need for the Ranbaxy brass to migrate from operations management to strategic management.

It took Athreya little time to discover the fantastic chemistry between Dr Singh and Brar. He realized that Brar was the company's most valuable asset. He was an extraordinary business leader, particularly brilliant in marketing insights and spotting global opportunities. Though not trained in medicinal chemistry, his knowledge of drugs not only in India but also in the rest of the world was equal to that of any specialist. Athreya also found that Brar would put a lot of constructive pressure on Dr Singh. He would share all his frustrations with his boss, challenging him to improve constantly. Dr Singh accepted all the pressure, as he knew it was in the best interests of the company. As a result, Ranbaxy brought about a host of improvements, especially in its market delivery systems.

By dint of sheer merit, Brar had risen to the second spot in the company after Dr Singh. Everybody knew that if Dr Singh were to step down one day, Brar would succeed him. For a while, Jag Mohan Khanna thought he was worthy of being Dr Singh's successor, thanks to the many successes in the field of research and development. However, he also gradually came round to the view that Brar was best suited for the job. In a global model for any pharmaceutical company, research and development cannot compete with business; its job is to aid business.

Athreya knew that if his plans for Ranbaxy's organizational restructuring had to see the light of the day, he would need somebody he could trust in the company. That is when he called up P.K. Sarangi. They had met while Athreya was on a consulting assignment for the public sector Indian Oil Corporation where Sarangi was working in the human resources development department. He had later joined Dunlop as vice-president, human resources. When Athreya spoke to him about shifting to Ranbaxy as in-charge of the human resource department, Sarangi was only too happy to join.

Athreya soon sensed that there were many people in the company who viewed his assignment with scepticism. Some felt that the pharmaceutical industry was different from other sectors and hence needed its own set of management principles. A few said that advanced business models apply only to multinationals and not to Indian business houses, while others said that an outsider like Athreya was not in a position to advise a pharmaceutical company. Athreya was hardly an outsider to the pharmaceutical industry, having consulted with drug companies like Glaxo and Sandoz in India as well as abroad.

Widespread scepticism made him realize that the top Ranbaxy managers would have to be involved in restructuring the company. Without that they would be reluctant to go along with the changes he had in mind. He started meeting the executive committee members individually to understand their assessment of the emerging scenario in the pharmaceutical industry, their perception of Ranbaxy's strengths and weaknesses and their own goals and ambitions. He then interacted with the other senior and mid-level managers, organizing workshops for them at Agra and Jaipur to assess their capabilities as well as to hear them voice their fears and apprehensions. By the end of it, he had a good idea of the talent available in the company.

By now, India had become a member of the WTO and was committed to reintroducing a product patent regime by 1 January 2005. In order to survive in the new environment, Ranbaxy had to transform itself into a research-based pharmaceutical company with its own drugs and delivery platforms. Given the huge investments in research and development required for this task, the company would have to look beyond India for its products. The country with just 1.2 per cent share of the world market for pharmaceutical products was just not large enough to sustain any worthwhile investment in research and development.

Athreya also drove home the point that people will increasingly spend more on their health. Expenditure will get diverted from food to healthcare products like vitamins. Ranbaxy needed to focus on the demands and expectations of the global, and not just the Indian, customer. Thus was born Ranbaxy's mission of becoming an international research-based pharmaceutical company. The roadmap drawn for the company was very clear: it would graduate from bulk drugs to generics and finally to its own proprietary products.

Athreya now needed to set a target for the company by giving it a vision. The target had to be fixed in such a way as to keep three sets of stakeholders in the company happy: the shareholders (so that they could see the value of their investments soar), the employees (in order to attract more talent) and the global customer. All three deserved a very challenging target. After lengthy discussions, a target of sales worth $1 billion by 2004 was set from around $200 million in 1994.

Much before the country's information technology companies made it fashionable to talk about their figures in dollars (more because of the stock exchange listing requirements in the United States than anything else) Ranbaxy had decided to record its turnover in a global currency. This was a bold move; it was known at that time that the Indian rupee would slide against the dollar for many years to come, making the target bigger in rupees.

Ranbaxy was now on its way to changing from an Indian company which exported to the world to becoming a global company with operations in India. Its organizational structure had to be in line with its new mission and vision and it had to adopt the culture of a multinational corporation.

By now, it was decided that Ranbaxy would focus on four markets: the United States, Europe, Asia Pacific and India. Athreya suggested an organizational structure to suit this shift in mindset. Each of the four markets would be headed by a regional director, with country managers reporting to him. Each regional director would report to the executive committee. Athreya also suggested that top executives be inducted into the board of directors to strengthen it and provide better strategic inputs. Soon Brar and Khanna were co-opted into the board, followed by Kaul and Sheth.

The company fixed the retirement age at fifty-eight years. In order to strengthen the management team and put in place a foolproof succession plan, Athreya selected thirty managers in the twenty-eight to thirty-five years age group and placed them in key positions after a thorough assessment of their capabilities. As the company was expanding overseas, it was also decided to hire local talent in other countries. Between 1993 and 1996, the number of foreigners working for Ranbaxy increased from 165 to 425.

Till the early-1990s, Ranbaxy had focussed on anti-infective drugs and had emerged as the country's largest player in this segment. However, anti-infective drugs were at the bottom of the value chain in the global markets. In the developed markets, there was a higher demand for drugs in the therapeutic segments like cardiovascular diseases, central nervous system disorders and skin problems, the so-called lifestyle drugs. If Ranbaxy had to grow in the developed markets, it would need to come out with products in these segments. This led to the company starting work on the development of statins, a new category of drugs used in treating cardiovascular ailments.

Ranbaxy was also considering acquisitions in order to strengthen its portfolio of products. A year after it acquired Gufic for its amoxycillin brand, Mox, in 1995, it also bought Mumbai-based Croslands Laboratories in an all-stock deal Ranbaxy found it was absent in the orthopaedics and dermatology segments of the market, two fast-growing areas. The Croslands portfolio included Volini for pain management and Fucibet, Fucidin and Silverex in the dermatology segment. Ranbaxy knew Croslands was up for sale and that Ajay Piramal, chairman of Nicholas Piramal India who had stunned the corporate world with a string of daring acquisitions around that time, was also in the race. It beat Piramal to get Croslands in 1996.

Finally, a new Ranbaxy was in place. In his address to the shareholders of the company in 1996, Dr Singh said:

> As the old guard gives in to more recent paradigms, they implant loud change that is profoundly revolutionary. These changes challenge all our erstwhile assumptions, old ways of thinking, bygone dogmas and yesterday's ideologies. No matter how cherished or how useful these were in the past, there is a clear consensus that they will not deliver in the present, let alone the future. Corporations respond to these challenges perforce through a series of transitions aimed at repositioning for the rapidly altering scenario of competition. The world as one large marketplace is no longer in the realm of economic ideology. We stand at the edge of fundamental shifts in human history where asking fundamental questions about our future is not so much a matter of intellectual curiosity as it is of survival.

Ranbaxy was now all set to embark on its global journey.

*

Flush with funds from the cefaclor deal with Eli Lilly in 1992, the company decided to add to its war chest. It raised $100 million by issuing global depository receipts. Rapid investments were made in setting up a global infrastructure. All told, the company had lined up investments worth $85 million in its various overseas ventures.

In Canada, Ranbaxy first initiated talks with Apothecon for a possible joint venture. However, it turned out to be a very ambitious company like Ranbaxy. It wanted the United States rights for all products developed jointly. But Ranbaxy was eyeing the United States market on its own and was only looking at Canada as a convenient entry point into the United States. Canadian products were well accepted in the United States and approvals from the USFDA came easily. Talks with Apothecon broke down and Ranbaxy initiated negotiations with Genpharm Inc., one of Canada's top twenty pharmaceutical companies. Genpharm Inc. is one of the many affiliated companies that comprise the worldwide group of Merck Generics, a subsidiary of Merck KGaA, world's oldest pharmaceutical company.

In August 1993, Ranbaxy formed a fifty-fifty joint venture with Genpharm, called Ranbaxy Genpharm Ltd. This company went on to acquire a manufacturing facility for oral cephalosporin formulations. Though this facility had the approval of the Canadian Health Protection Branch, Ranbaxy set about upgrading it to meet USFDA standards since the plant was supposed to supply cefaclor to the American market.

But the marketing joint venture with Eli Lilly meant there was no need to reach cefaclor to the United States through a circuitous route. Also, Ranbaxy found it difficult to meet the Genpharm CEO, who was constantly travelling as his business interests were spread across North America, Europe and Africa. As a result, the joint venture was folded up.

Ranbaxy had also identified Ireland as a possible manufacturing base. Ireland had emerged as a low-cost producer of drugs and most pharmaceutical companies had set up shop there. Though Ranbaxy had exported pharmaceutical products to the United Kingdom, it knew that regulatory approvals for such exports would take a lot of time. A facility in Ireland, it was felt, would be the best way to enter the United Kingdom.

Ranbaxy zeroed in on Rima Labs, a small company located at Cashel, some 120 km south-west of Dublin. This company had several products in its portfolio, including liquids and veterinary medicine, and a number of licensed products for the United Kingdom market, though none of them was big. Soon after acquiring the unit, Ranbaxy stopped the manufacture of liquids and animal-health products, as these were not a part of its core strengths. More importantly, Ranbaxy now had a certified quality control laboratory and was able to access the entire European Union by routing its products through this laboratory.

Ranbaxy also got the much-needed foothold in the generics market in the United Kingdom. As in the United States, retailers in the United Kingdom did not entertain companies with a limited range of products, preferring to deal with those who had a complete portfolio of drugs. This acquisition helped Ranbaxy put together a bouquet of products for the market.

Ranbaxy now got down to acquiring a similar production unit in the United States. Hemant Shah, a New Jersey-based drug analyst, had been making waves in that country in the 1990s and had been rated the best drug analyst for two successive years. In 1995, Brar contacted Shah and set up a meeting with him over dinner. At the meeting, Brar asked Shah to guide Ranbaxy in the United States. Shah was moved. He had left India many years ago and, he said, it was his dream to bring at least one Indian company to the United States. Though he was associated more with research-based companies than generic companies, he agreed to become Ranbaxy's associate in the United States.

In September 1995, Ranbaxy had acquired a 100 per cent stake in Ohm's Labs for $12 million from a group of non-resident Indian physicians led by Ashok Lohadia and Arun Heble. At the time of acquisition, the company had sixty-five employees and a turnover of $8 million in over-the-counter products. But what was more important was the fact that it had a clean track record with no warnings from the USFDA.

Over the years, Ranbaxy emerged as a leading pharmaceutical company in several overseas markets. In the United States, it became the fastest company to record sales of $100 million and was declared the fastest-growing pharmaceutical company in 2001. By the end of 2003, it was amongst the top ten generic pharmaceutical companies in the United States. In Brazil, too, it had emerged as the fastest-growing pharmaceutical company by 2002 and achieved the highest growth of 37 per cent amongst the top 100 pharmaceutical companies in that country. The company's overall ranking in the country improved from fifty-three in 2001 to thirty-seven in 2002. Its market share in the generic segment moved up from 9.3 per cent in December 2001 to 14.78 per cent in November 2002, putting it amongst the top five generic companies in the country.

By 2002, Ranbaxy also became the leading pharmaceutical company in Myanmar and was ranked as the third-largest branded generic company in the Nigerian pharmaceutical market. It was amongst the top five pharmaceutical companies in Sri Lanka, while it was ranked fourteenth in the Malaysian market. In generic pharmaceuticals, it was amongst the top ten companies in Malaysia.

In Vietnam, where its overall ranking improved from nineteen in 2001 to fourteen in 2002, Ranbaxy recorded the highest growth of 47 per cent amongst the top twenty pharmaceutical companies. It was placed amongst the top five players in the country in the generics space. The company became the second-largest player in anti-retroviral products in 2002. It ranked number one in terms of new product launches in the country and three of its products were among the top twenty launches during 2002. Ranbaxy was ranked thirty amongst foreign companies in China and forty-two in Thailand in 2002.

But it was its presence in the American market that was the feather in Ranbaxy's cap. Deepak Chattaraj was to play a crucial role in this.

*

Deepak Chattaraj had come to Ranbaxy in April 1991 from the State Trading Corporation, the government-owned international trading house. Chattaraj had been involved with the export of medicine from India, working closely with the country's leading drug companies. While in the State Trading Corporation, he had formed a consortium of Indian pharmaceutical companies for exports to developing countries like Sudan and Sri Lanka against government tenders. In 1982, Chattaraj had been posted in London for five years, which helped him closely study the regulatory environment in the United Kingdom as well as the United States.

By 1991, the State Trading Corporation was on a decline as the government had opened up imports. By now it had also occurred to Chattaraj that after making a success out of bulk drug exports, some Indian companies were ready to take the next step and enter the formulations segment of the developed markets. He decided to leave the Corporation and sign up with one of these companies. He sent out feelers to a host of companies, but joined Ranbaxy as it was most eager to seize opportunities abroad. What also influenced Chattaraj was Ranbaxy's success in making cefaclor.

Ranbaxy had opened an office at Raleigh in North Carolina as soon as it was certain that the doors to the United States market had opened, thanks to the tie-up with Eli Lilly. It appointed James Youmans, who had earlier worked for Glaxo and Eli Lilly, as president of its American operations. By now, Ranbaxy had also struck a deal with Schein to supply ranitidine. Just as it started studying the local regulatory environment in greater detail, Youmans decided to leave and join Sandoz. As things were moving at a brisk pace, Chattaraj was sent to Raleigh in January 1996 to take over as officiating president. By September, Ranbaxy realized that Chattaraj was doing a fine job and he was confirmed as president.

In August 1996, when Dr Singh had come to the United States to leave his elder son, Malvinder, at Duke University at Raleigh, he asked Chattaraj to fix up a meeting with Randy Toubouis, the executive chairman of Eli Lilly, and his deputy, Sydney Taurel. The two agreed to meet their Indian business partners over lunch at the penthouse of their plush office at Indianapolis. On the assigned date, Dr Singh and Chattaraj flew out of Raleigh for the meeting, their spirits soaring. But the two were in for a rude shock, when they were told over lunch that Eli Lilly was no longer interested in generic medicine, as there weren't enough profits to be made to attract a research-based company like Eli Lilly. Though Ranbaxy had sensed some coldness on Eli Lilly's part since late-1995, it was not prepared for this.

Ranbaxy had failed to anticipate some developments. By mid-1996, it was clear that President Clinton would not be able to push through his promise of cheap medicine for all by encouraging the generics companies. As a result, Big Pharma instantly lost interest in generics. Though the reasons for Eli Lilly backing out of the venture were not specifically spelt out, it had started developing some sort of a relationship with another American generic company, Mylan Laboratories. Seeing better prospects with this company, Eli Lilly decided to call off its alliance with Ranbaxy.

This not only meant the end of the American joint venture, it also made the research and development joint venture in India almost redundant as it was set up only to develop a pipeline of generic products for the United States market. Further negotiations drove home the point that there was no way Eli Lilly would reconsider its decision.

Badly shaken by the announcement, Dr Singh and Chattaraj prepared to return to Raleigh. At the Indianapolis airport, Dr Singh quizzed Chattaraj about how he felt. 'Look at it this way,' Chattaraj told his boss, 'Ranbaxy would have done all the donkey's work in the collaboration, while all profits would have to be shared 50 per cent with Eli Lilly. I have studied the United States market and I know that Ranbaxy can do well on its own. It is good riddance.

Let's see it as an opportunity.' Though it took Ranbaxy some time to recover from the shock, this was precisely the course it took.

Back in India, the company explored three options: seek a new partner in the United States, set up a base on its own or retreat into a supply model, feeding the American market out of exports from India. After debating the issue internally for a few months, it was decided that the company would go to the United States on its own. The issues that needed to be addressed were how Ranbaxy should go about it and how it could leverage the Eli Lilly connection to launch itself in the United States.

The first product for which Ranbaxy got USFDA approval was cefaclor. Though the application was submitted in November 1995, the approval came only in August 1997. Ranbaxy launched cefaclor, its first prescription product in the United States, in January 1998. But it was next to impossible for a single-product company to find a space in the medical stores. For that, Ranbaxy needed a whole portfolio of drugs.

Around this time, Ranbaxy was discussing the terms of its disengagement with Eli Lilly. After snapping its ties, Eli Lilly had told Ranbaxy that it was willing to compensate for the pain and distress caused. When the two companies had formed the joint venture, Eli Lilly had been a little wary of Ranbaxy's fidelity. Perhaps it was aware that before the tie-up, top Ranbaxy functionaries had been meeting whoever was willing to give them an appointment. Besides, this was also the first time that Eli Lilly was doing business with an Indian company. As a result, it had insisted on inserting a five-year no-divorce clause in the joint venture agreement. Several advisers told Dr Singh that Ranbaxy could make money out of this clause. Some said the company could get up to $100 million, though the consensus was that Eli Lilly could easily be asked to fork out $25–30 million. Between Dr Singh and Brar, they knew that the company could easily make $5–10 million, no small change for Ranbaxy at the time.

Instead, in a carefully calculated move, Ranbaxy asked for eight Eli Lilly products. These products were over thirty years old and had combined sales of less than $5 million. Eli Lilly had flogged these products for long and had no interest left. Chattaraj and his men handpicked the drugs after a careful study; though these were off-patent and old drugs, there were no other producers of these medicines anywhere in the world. At that time, Eli Lilly was the only producer in the world of medicines like tincture of opium, used in the treatment of stomach pain and ulcers. A month after launching cefaclor, Ranbaxy launched these eight Eli Lilly products in the United States.

In hindsight, it proved to be the wisest decision Ranbaxy ever made. Till then, it had been supplying bulk cefaclor to Eli Lilly, which was selling the product under its own label. After leasing the eight products to Ranbaxy, Eli Lilly sent letters to all its wholesalers saying that these drugs would henceforth be supplied by Ranbaxy. All of a sudden, the wholesalers in the United States became aware of the Ranbaxy name. What could have taken years and millions of dollars to accomplish, was done with this one letter. Ranbaxy had made its move after careful consideration. Before inking the deal with Eli Lilly, the company had met a number of wholesalers in the United States only to be told that the space for generic medicine was saturated and they were unwilling to stock another label, least of all an unheard one called Ranbaxy. The deal ensured that Ranbaxy had a readymade platform with the dealers. In addition, Ranbaxy got Eli Lilly to lend its name to the labels as wholesalers as well as consumers did not want a stand-alone Ranbaxy label.

The final deal was signed by Brar in Singapore on 19 May 1997, less than a week after Dr Singh was detected with cancer of the oesophagus. It was with a heavy heart that Brar signed on the dotted line. Dr Singh's illness was still a carefully guarded secret with only a handful of people aware of it. There was nobody Brar could have spoken to in order to lighten his burden. Cutting short a trip to Saigon (Ho Chi Minh City), Brar returned to Delhi and was on a flight to the United States two days later to look up his boss, friend and mentor.

By 1998, Ranbaxy was in business in the United States with its cefaclor and the eight Eli Lilly products. In July 2000, Ranbaxy acquired the brand Proctosol from Signature for $8 million—the payment was to be staggered over a period of time—in order to understand the market better. The acquisition was supposed to give the company insights into the marketing of a branded drug in the US. Proctosol, at that time, had annual sales of $4.5 million.

There were other risks that Ranbaxy took in the United States market. When it got to know that cephalexin was a big product, it decided to source the product from Eli Lilly, rather than wait for its own cephalexin, which would have to be cleared by the USFDA. Whenever a drug goes off-patent, generic players get into a race to launch the drug. The first mover's advantage is crucial as prices take a tumble right away. Ranbaxy bought cephalexin 500 mg from Eli Lilly at $45 per pack and sold it at $37—recording a loss of $8 on every pack. Ranbaxy was aware that Barr and Apothecon (the generics arm of Bristol Myers-Squibb, which was acquired by Geneva Pharmaceuticals in 2000) had decided to exit from the cephalexin market, because of the low profit margins. It also knew that Teva was keen on launching the product. So it got into an agreement with Teva to supply the drug. Though this resulted in a loss of $2.5–3 million during the first year, it helped Ranbaxy attain a critical mass. The company then entered into a deal with United States-based Ivax to source cephalexin at $39, which reduced its losses. Soon, Ranbaxy's own cephalexin was ready to be launched in the United States. With its own product, the company was able to recover its losses many times over.

Ranbaxy's American business recorded a turnover of $15 million in 1998, the first year of operations. The turnover rose to $33 million in 1999, $65 million in 2000 (the year Ranbaxy broke even) and $113 million in 2001. No other generics company had breached the $100 million mark as fast as Ranbaxy—in four years flat, and that too with a comfortable profit margin.

Ranbaxy was extremely careful about selecting the products to launch in the United States. It picked up products where there was very little competition from other generic companies. The three products it launched in 2001—twice-a-day amoxycillin, minocycline 75 mg, clindamycin 300 mg—gave the company virtual monopoly in the generics space. This not only gave the company high sales but also good profits.

Chattaraj had come to realize early that Ranbaxy could not be successful in the United States if it continued with Indian business practices. Doing business over fax would lead to many business partners questioning Ranbaxy's credentials. Digital connectivity was a must. So Ranbaxy implemented the SAP enterprise resource planning software at a time when it was bleeding in the United States.

The termination of the Eli Lilly deal put a question mark on Ranbaxy's carefully drawn up plans of becoming an international company. Though the investments had been made, the returns had not come. Several markets including China, Indonesia, Poland and South Africa did not respond in the manner that they were projected to. Investors had started doubting the Ranbaxy model. For a moment, it seemed that Dr Singh's detractors were ready to hit back at him for not heeding his father. Bhai Mohan Singh had opposed the frenetic growth plans drawn up by Dr Singh and Brar. Now, Dr Singh was very close to being proved wrong. Investors had started saying that instead of choosing to become a multinational, it would have been better if Ranbaxy had chosen to export out of India. A less ambitious model would fetch better returns for the company, they argued.

Actually, Ranbaxy was in a bind. Having made a commitment to go global, there was no way it could have pulled back its investments. Till 1998, Ranbaxy was left with no choice but to prop up its earnings through treasury operations—a practice that was stopped once the returns on the company's overseas investments started flowing in. Treasury operations first made a sizeable contribution to the company's bottom line in 1994-95. Out of a total profit of Rs 110 crore for the year, Rs 21 crore came from other income, largely from the sale of investments. Next year, other income accounted for Rs 33.4 crore, while profit after tax stood at Rs 135 crore.

This soon sucked Ranbaxy into a controversy—the stock market scam of 2001.

*

The key player in this scam was Ketan Parekh, a stockbroker who had, by the late-1990s, emerged as the 'big bull' of the Indian stock markets, betting heavily on technology companies. The price of any scrip he touched would soon shoot up through the roof and the KP stocks, as they came to be known, were a sure bet for any investor. Parekh's reputation as Mr Moneybags grew by the day, till he was brought down by a bear cartel.

The thirty-share bellwether index of the Bombay Stock Exchange (BSE), Sensex, had shown sharp fluctuations during the early months of 2001. From around 4,000 points in the beginning of January, it had risen to 4,437 on 15 February before coming down to 4,069 on 27 February, the day before the Union budget. On 28 February, the budget day, it rose by 177 points and closed at 4,247 points. The next day, it again rose by 24 points to 4,271 points. But on 2 March, the Sensex fell by 176 points, with a number of leading scrips showing high volatility. The same day, the Securities & Exchange Board of India (SEBI), the stock market watchdog, instituted an inquiry into the whole affair.

Soon, the matter was raised in the Parliament, with several members of Parliament (MPs) insisting that certain brokers had acted in collusion with banks in the rise of the Sensex and that public funds were in jeopardy because of the fall. Their worst fears proved true on 8 March, when there were indications that a payment crisis was looming large over the Calcutta Stock Exchange as some big brokers had defaulted on their pay-in obligations.

The next day, there was a run on the Madhavpura Mercantile Cooperative Bank, the second largest bank in the state of Gujarat, fuelled by rumours that the bank had given large sums of money to Parekh for investing in the stock markets and that, with the fall in share prices, a large part of this money had been wiped out. Investors rushed to the Ahmedabad branch of the bank to withdraw their deposits. On 13 March, the bank closed down all its branches saying it could no longer meet its liabilities.

Alarmed at the public outcry, a thirty-member Joint Parliamentary Committee (JPC) was constituted to inquire into the developments. Even as the committee had begun its probe, another crisis surfaced which showed that the rot ran very deep. On 2 July, the public sector Unit Trust of India (UTI), the country's oldest and largest fund manager, declared that it was suspending redemptions from its US 64 fund till the end of the year. The announcement sent tremors in the financial markets. UTI was the single largest investor in the stock market, controlling assets worth Rs 60,000 crore. Its US 64 fund accounted for 15 per cent of the total assets of the mutual fund industry at that time. The next day, the UTI chairman was asked to leave and the Central Bureau of

Investigation slapped a case against him and three others for causing wrongful losses to UTI by making imprudent investments.

Soon, skeletons started tumbling out of various cupboards. Parekh told the JPC that in 1999-2000, the companies alleged to be connected or associated with him reported profits of Rs 215 crore and paid income tax of about Rs 100 crore. This, he said, had boosted his confidence levels and he started building up huge positions in the market which required him to make large financial commitments. 'In the hope that my bullishness for India and Indian technology companies will come true, I crossed the principles of risk management and failed miserably,' he admitted. During 2000-01, interest in technology scrips started losing flavour the world over with fears of a recession setting in and all markets across the globe went into a bear phase. He said that since he was a large investor and had grossly over-committed himself to the market, many market players started taking advantage of the situation. 'In order to honour my commitments, I raised resources from banks by pledging assets, from corporates by selling my investments and from market intermediaries etc., which, instead of reducing my financial burden, actually deepened the crisis,' he said.

In the course of investigations by SEBI, it came to light that one of the companies that had lent money to Parekh was Vidyut Investments, a subsidiary of Ranbaxy. It was common practice amongst companies at that time to provide their surplus cash to stockbrokers against securities of shares. In keeping with the trend, Ranbaxy, seeking to improve its financials through treasury income, also gave some money to brokerage firms belonging to Parekh. However, it had stipulated that the money should not be used to dabble in the Ranbaxy stock—letters to this effect were recovered by SEBI from Parekh's offices. At that time, there were no indications that Parekh was doing anything improper.

However, Parekh had in fact dealt in Ranbaxy shares. Investigators came across evidence that some Parekh companies had done circular trade amongst themselves and with other broking groups like Credit Suisse First Boston to create an artificial market in the scrip. But when the bull run happened and Ranbaxy shares also shot up, Parekh had already liquidated his holding in the company and was left with only 1,500 shares. Parekh had sold his Ranbaxy shares in the fourth quarter of 1999 while the bull run took place in 2000. There was no evidence that he had used Ranbaxy money to buy Ranbaxy shares.

But the company could not escape the Parekh effect. When the markets fell, Ranbaxy was left with no option but to liquidate the shares Parekh had given as a security. However, their value had greatly diminished. All told, the company's bottom line was affected to the tune of Rs 30–32 crore. Subsequently, in 2001, the company made it a policy to stop financing stockbrokers.

9

A Legend Passes Away

One evening in May 1997, at around 5.30 p.m., O.P. Sood bumped into Dr Singh at Ranbaxy's Nehru Place office. Dr Singh called him over to his room, where Brar was already present. While looking at his papers, Dr Singh mentioned that he had a problem in swallowing food and, at times, felt nauseous after a meal. He didn't look concerned at all.

Sood told him that this could be because of some obstruction in the food canal and suggested a barium swallow to find out the cause. Dr Singh agreed and asked Sood to schedule a test at 10 a.m. the next day. Sood called up his radiologist friend, Sudershan Agarwal, who ran the Dewan Chand Agarwal medical centre in the heart of New Delhi, and arranged for the test.

Around noon the next day, Sood got a call from Agarwal who sounded very worried. Though he had given some vague answers to Dr Singh, the radiologist told Sood that the test pointed to a cancerous growth in the oesophagus and suggested an immediate endoscopy to rule out cancer.

A shell-shocked Sood immediately left his office at Gurgaon for Nehru Place and barged into Dr Singh's office. Before he could say a word, Dr Singh knew from the expression on his face that all was not well. Staying as calm as he could, Sood told him what Agarwal had said. Dr Singh immediately called Brar to his office and apprised him of the situation. After asking Sood a few questions, Brar asked him to keep the findings a secret. It was also decided to go in for an endoscopy immediately.

Sood now called another friend, Professor S.K. Sarin at the Govind Ballabh Pant hospital, who agreed to carry out the endoscopy. By 9.30 a.m. the next day, he confirmed that it was cancer. Subsequently, a biopsy was carried out which also showed that the tissue was cancerous. Dr Singh had cancer of the lower oesophagus and stomach. Though it was still at an early stage, the doctors gave him only two years more to live.

It was time to act fast. Sood immediately placed a phone call to Dr P.S. Joshi at Beas, asking him to rush to Delhi. Dr Joshi, after all, was no ordinary doctor.

*

Dr Singh with wife Nimmi and sons Malvinder and Shivinder.

After getting an MBBS from Amritsar and an MD specializing in cardiology from the Govind Ballabh Pant hospital in New Delhi, Dr Joshi worked in the United Kingdom and the United States, where he had a flourishing practice. However, unhappy with the healthcare system in the United States, he returned to India in the late 1970s and teamed up with Rajan Nanda of the Escorts group and began working at the hospital set up at the Escorts factory in Faridabad, on the outskirts of Delhi.

In the mid-1980s, Rajan Nanda's father, H.P. Nanda, had decided to set up a charitable hospital in Delhi, specializing in heart diseases. Dr Joshi was now roped in to play a key role in the new venture. However, even before the hospital could start functioning, Dr Joshi left Escorts, much to Rajan Nanda's consternation. Meanwhile, Chandra Kant Birla, a member of the prominent Birla business family, had drawn up plans to build a hospital in Delhi and had chosen Dr Joshi to lead the venture, paying him very well. But there was no progress in the project and Dr Joshi asked Birla to cut his salary by half.

Around this time Dr Joshi was going through an emotional turmoil. He realized his healing powers were limited and would often feel helpless when patients came to him from far-off places, expecting him to perform miracles. The question bothering him was how much should a doctor charge his patients. Charging too little would make the patient indebted to the doctor; but too high a fee would put the doctor into the patient's debt. Soon, Dr Joshi had left the Birla venture and started out on his own, charging only Rs 5 as consultation fees. Medicine, he had come to realize, was to be practised to relieve people from their pains and not for money.

He now embarked on his quest for inner peace. He tried to contact various spiritual leaders and movements, among others, Swami Paramhansa Yogananda (the author of *Autobiography of a Yogi*), disciples of Swami

Ramakrishna Paramhansa and Swami Muktananda. However, he either failed to make any headway or found that the flame lit by the saints had faded. He had also read numerous books written by Osho Rajneesh, the modern guru, but was disillusioned by the controversies surrounding him. H.P. Nanda's family followed the teachings of the nineteenth-century saint, Sai Baba of Shirdi, but Dr Joshi wanted someone in flesh and blood who could answer the questions tormenting him. Nanda's wife then suggested that Dr Joshi should visit Beas and meet the Maharaj Ji, which he did in late-1984. His search had ended—Dr Joshi had found his spiritual guru.

The meeting solved all his problems. The Maharaj Ji asked him to take charge of the Beas hospital. This suited Dr Joshi fine; he could provide free medicine to his patients and leave it to the Maharaj Ji to decide his compensation. The multi-facility hospital at Beas had started off as a three-week eye camp held every quarter. *Sevadars* (volunteers) from the Radhasoami Satsang served at the camp as nurses. Some time in the mid-1980s, it was decided that the camp should be expanded into a full-fledged hospital with specialists for diseases like high blood pressure and heart ailments which afflicted a large number of people in and around Beas. The hospital grew, opening two more branches, one at Sikandarpur in Haryana and the other at Hamirpur in Himachal Pradesh. Soon, it was catering to a population of over 1.5 million and was funded to the extent of Rs 1 crore a month by the Radhasoami Satsang.

Dr Joshi had first met Dr Singh in the late 1970s, soon after his return to India, when he was attached to a nursing home in New Delhi. Manjit had fallen ill and Bhai Mohan Singh had summoned Dr Joshi to treat him. They then met after Dr Joshi had joined the Radhasoami Satsang and got to know each other well. Dr Joshi soon realized that Dr Singh was extremely serious about his work. Dr Joshi was well aware of the latest developments in the field of medicine and he found Dr Singh equally knowledgeable on the subject. He realized that Dr Singh had the capability to tap the right sources for information. The influence of the Radhasoami Satsang on Dr Singh was plainly visible—apart from being a vegetarian and a teetotaller, Dr Singh was honest to the core and a man of very strong convictions.

In the mid-1990s, the Maharaj Ji's brother was taken ill and was admitted to the Escorts Heart Institute in New Delhi. Dr Singh was organizing the import of certain medicines required for the treatment. As Dr Joshi was involved closely with the treatment, Dr Singh got to interact with him and was impressed with his knowledge of medicine. He then invited Dr Joshi to join the Ranbaxy board, making Dr Joshi the first practising doctor to join the board.

*

After Sood had spoken to him, Dr Joshi was in Delhi the next morning to take charge of the situation. In cancer, speed is vital for successful treatment. Within seventy-two hours of the diagnosis, Dr Singh and Dr Joshi had left for the Memorial Sloane-Kettering Cancer Center in New York. Dr Joshi was able to locate an Indian doctor, Manjit Singh Bains, at the hospital, who was an expert in cancer of the oesophagus. Though they had gone prepared for a surgery, Bains recommended chemotherapy first to destroy the cancerous growth. Subsequently, the affected parts of the oesophagus were removed through surgery. After reading up on the subject, Dr Joshi had come to know that only 20 per cent of those who had cancer of the oesophagus survive for more than a year but he hoped that the prompt treatment would lead to a different outcome in Dr Singh's case.

All this while, Dr Singh was aware that cancer was eating into his innards. But he was an exceptionally strong man. Dr Joshi realized that the whole treatment was just another project for Dr Singh; there was a problem at hand and a solution had to be found.

A few months after the surgery, it was found that Dr Singh had developed a secondary cancerous growth in the liver. As the primary cancer had been removed from the oesophagus, it was felt that if the affected part of the liver was removed, he could get a fresh lease of life. Dr Joshi sensed though that if a secondary growth had been detected in the liver, there could be a similar growth in other parts of his body as well. But a scan done in the United States had shown that the disease had spread only to the liver.

There were two options: either have a liver transplant done through a very complicated surgery or remove the affected part of the liver and let the organ grow back to its normal size over time. It was decided to go for the second option. Dr Joshi had located a hospital in Tokyo, which had earned a reputation for carrying out such operations. Four surgeons operated upon Dr Singh for over four hours. During the surgery, more spots of cancerous growth were detected and removed. Dr Singh responded well to the treatment and started recuperating fast.

Meanwhile, Dr Joshi had come to know about apoptosis genes—a set of codified instructions, which tell a cell to die. If these genes could somehow be injected into the cancer cells, their death could be triggered. This could check the spread of the cancer. Though it had not yet been developed into a treatment, it was an emerging area of research. He was informed that some doctors in Singapore had made considerable progress in this therapy. So Dr Joshi flew to Singapore, only to learn that the treatment was still in an experimental stage, with not enough clinical work done on it.

Dr Joshi also learnt of an institute in Hong Kong, which specialized in herbal treatment and took Dr Singh there. The doctors told them it was too late and nothing could be done. However, they prescribed a medicine which required some herbs to be boiled in water till it turned into a brackish liquid. Dr Singh found the concoction dreadful and could take it only with extreme difficulty. A physician from Dehradun, who claimed to make his own medicine, tried ayurvedic treatment but even that did not work.

In the end, Dr Singh was able to survive for two years, because the best treatment in the world was made available to him. He was never unduly perturbed at the prospect of death. The teachings of the Radhasoami Satsang had lifted him to a higher plane of existence.

*

The Radhasoami Satsang was started in the nineteenth century by Shiv Dayal Singh, who later came to be known as Soami Ji. Dr Singh's father-in-law, Charan Singh, became the leader of the Satsang in 1951 and came to be known as Maharaj Ji. The teachings of the Satsang are simple. It seeks to bring about a union of man and God through meditation. Drawing inspiration from Hindu as well as Muslim sages and mystics of the middle ages, it talks of eventually liberating the spirit from the cycle of birth and death for an ultimate reunion with the supreme being, which has neither any shape nor any form. Radhasoami is a combination of two words: Radha, the soul, and Swami, the master. In other words, a Satsangi is one who has mastered his soul. Everybody who is initiated into the Satsang needs to become a vegetarian for a year and is given a mantra by the master for meditation.

Dr Singh got initiated into the Satsang soon after his marriage and his spiritual nature helped him imbibe deeply from the teachings of the Satsang. He gave up non-vegetarian food and turned a teetotaller. He also developed a disdain for luxuries and took to a very simple lifestyle. He ate very simple food and showed no indulgences of any kind. He was also extremely close to his father-in-law. He would take his wife and two sons to Beas regularly and the whole family would participate in voluntary labour, mingling with everybody else. The two men also shared a love for photography, with both of them spending hours together to get the right shade and colours for their pictures.

Dr Singh was shaken when Maharaj Ji died in 1991. He was in Moscow at that time and the family was able to reach him with a lot of difficulty. He rushed back to Delhi and headed straight for Beas from the airport, along with his mother and was silent throughout the journey. There were strong rumours that he would succeed Maharaj Ji as the leader of the Satsang, which did not happen. When Dr Singh was diagnosed with cancer many years later, another rumour started doing the rounds that the Maharaj Ji may have been aware that Dr Singh did not have long to live and that is why he chose not to appoint him as his successor.

Dr Singh also instilled in his sons the same values and ideals of simplicity. Though he adored both of them, he could also be strict. At dinner, for instance, the whole family had to sit together and eat whatever was served. He never approved of them watching Hindi films or holding lengthy telephone conversations. He was very particular about how the boys used their time. In school, the children were forbidden from taking expensive stuff along and were told to make do with whatever was prescribed. Bimal Raizada had once travelled with Dr Singh to Dehradun. There, Dr Singh went to meet his sons, while Raizada went on to Mussoorie in the company car. Once there, he was surprised to find Dr Singh and his two sons alight at the bus stand in a rickety state transport corporation bus.

It was his belief in the teachings of the Radhasoami that kept Dr Singh in good cheer during his illness. A disease can peel off the masks people wear. Many successful people have an aura of energy and control till their potency is challenged by a terminal ailment. But nothing about Dr Singh changed. Never did he give the impression of being a broken man. Even when he knew his days were numbered, he would say 'perfect' in a booming voice whenever somebody asked him how he was feeling. He never solicited sympathy, not even from his own children. With his close friends, he behaved as if nothing had happened.

Because of chemotherapy, he had lost most of his beard. Yet, he was not ashamed of it, nor did he ever make attempts to hide his illness. In early-1998, he had gone to Ranbaxy's factory at Dewas. At dinner at Pushpinder Bindra's, somebody inquired about his health, only to have Dr Singh reply, 'My beard is growing back. I must be fine.' It was this attitude which led many to believe that he would beat the odds and survive the cancer. A few months before his death, Dr Singh had thrown a party. There was very little hair left on his face. Everybody was embarrassed, except Dr Singh. He mingled with the guests and never gave the impression of a man on his deathbed.

Three months before his death in July 1999, he called up Bindra at Dewas with a request. Dr Singh's cook of twenty years had decided to leave; could the cook at Ranbaxy's guest house at Indore be sent across to Delhi? Till the last, Dr Singh was unwilling to give up on life.

Once, when his friend Surendra Daulat Singh's wife asked him why he didn't ask his spiritual master to intercede, Dr Singh said, after brooding over the question for a while: 'The master is doing what is the best for me.' He demonstrated how a man could depart from the world at the peak of his life with dignity.

Sood's wife had developed an ovarian cancer in end-1998 and was constantly in and out of hospital. Though he was very weak by then, Dr Singh would climb several flights of stairs to see her in Sood's second-floor house. On 3 July 1999, she was admitted to the Indraprastha Apollo Hospital in Delhi for treatment. There Sood happened to meet Malvinder who told him that his father was in the hospital's intensive care unit (ICU). Sood rushed to the ICU to see his ailing boss. He found him in full control of his senses, talking on his cellphone. He inquired about Sood's wife and said that he would call them over to his new farmhouse soon. Two days later, he was dead. But not before he had carried out his responsibilities.

*

Once word spread that Dr Singh was suffering from a terminal ailment, there were concerns about Ranbaxy's future. Who would succeed him? Like most progressive businessmen, Dr Singh knew that his job was not only to strategize but also to ensure ethical corporate governance in the company. The first role was that of a CEO and the second that of a chairman. He had been wearing both hats. But it was clear to him that as Ranbaxy would expand, it would be difficult for his successor to carry out both the responsibilities. This required the posts of chairman and CEO to be separated. As a result, he not only had to find a new chief executive for Ranbaxy, he also had to find a chairman—somebody worthy of slipping into his shoes.

Dr Singh had such a person in mind. Towards the end of April 1998, he called on the Lt. Governor of Delhi, Tejinder Khanna, at his residence. Khanna was to retire shortly and Dr Singh wanted him to join the Ranbaxy board of directors. Khanna agreed and joined Ranbaxy in September 1998.

Dr Singh and Khanna had a long association. Khanna's father, K.L. Khanna, was the secretary of the Radhasoami Satsang at Beas. Khanna, a 1961-batch IAS officer from the Punjab cadre, was initiated into the faith in 1960 and was present at Dr Singh's wedding. More than the Radhasoami Satsang connection, it was Khanna's reputation as an upright bureaucrat during his long career of over thirty-seven years that appealed to Dr Singh.

Khanna's work first got noticed during his tenure as the

managing director of the Punjab State Industrial Development Corporation (PSIDC) from 1969 to 1972. The state had just embarked on the Green Revolution, and farm mechanization was happening at a fast pace. There was a great demand for tractors and the need for producing tractors within the state was keenly felt.

Khanna came to know that the government-owned Central Mechanical Engineering Research Institute (CMERI) at Durgapur in West Bengal had developed a tractor prototype called Swaraj. However, the government had rejected the prototype while scouting for technology for the public sector Hindustan Machine Tools Ltd. Khanna was convinced that the CMERI technology would work and, putting his career at stake, got PSIDC to set up Punjab Tractors to commercialize the venture. The gamble paid off and Swaraj went on to become a leading tractor brand in the country, while Punjab Tractors became a blue-chip at the stock market.

Over the next two decades, Khanna's reputation as an honest and sincere bureaucrat grew. In 1992, as the Food Secretary in the Central government, he was able to avert a major food shortage crisis and also save the country valuable foreign exchange.

That year, the wheat crop had failed in north India and the country needed to import three million tones of wheat to stave off a crisis. However, whenever India announced that it was entering a commodity market as a buyer, prices would shoot up. Since the country's foreign exchange reserves were extremely low at the time, any such development would have spelled disaster. Imports, therefore, had to be done in utmost secrecy. Dr Manmohan Singh, the finance minister, brought Khanna in from Punjab in March 1992 to handle the sensitive project.

Immediately on taking charge, Khanna first contacted the Canadian government, holding out an implicit threat to tap the American market if prices were not reasonable. The trick worked and Canada agreed to sell one million tonnes of wheat to India. Khanna next approached the Australian government, which refused, saying that it had contracted all its wheat for the year. But when Australia realized that India had paid Canada in cash for the wheat, it reverted, saying that Iraq had cancelled its order and it could sell one million tonnes of wheat to India. Since they were now in a weaker position, Khanna managed to drive a hard bargain.

He still needed to procure another one million tonnes and decided to tap the American market. Khanna knew that the United States Agricultural Department gave an export enhancement subsidy. So he asked the Indian ambassador to the United States, Abid Hussain, to make inquiries and check this as well. Hussain's feedback was far from encouraging: the United States would not give the subsidy to India since it had trade relations with Cuba. Luckily for Khanna, it was election year in the United States and the George Bush administration did not want to antagonize the powerful farm lobby. The American ambassador to India, Thomas Pickering, sent an envoy to Khanna asking him to buy American wheat. Khanna clinched the deal. All told, Khanna's efforts saved the country at least $65 million. And it did not involve any expensive overseas visits by bureaucrats—it was all done over the phone on Khanna's desk.

Khanna went on to become the Union Commerce Secretary. Towards the end of 1996, when he was close to retirement, Dr Singh first asked him to join the Ranbaxy board. Khanna agreed but could not take up the assignment as he was made the Lt. Governor of Delhi. Dr Singh waited for one and a half years and made the offer again when Khanna was all set to give up the Lt. Governor's job.

There was another role Dr Singh had in mind for Khanna. Towards the end of April 1999, Dr Singh called Khanna for a meeting at his farmhouse. He was all alone and was looking very sick. He said that he wanted to set up a trust to look after the interests of his family and he wanted Khanna to be a trustee.

Nobody had any doubts about who would succeed Dr Singh as the CEO. Brar had enough achievements to his credit to lead Ranbaxy. He had amassed tremendous knowledge of the global pharmaceutical market and was an inspiring leader. Moreover, Dr Singh was convinced that Brar was the best brain in the Indian pharmaceutical industry.

But there was a small hitch. Brar was unwilling to continue in the corporate world for too long. On 14 March 1997, at a party at Ranbaxy's Sunder Nagar guest house to celebrate Brar's completing twenty years with the company, he had announced that he would leave as soon as he turned fifty to pursue something that didn't confine him to a nine-to-five job. There were over fifty people present at the party and Brar had said it in all seriousness. But this was before Dr Singh was diagnosed with cancer.

Dr Singh's illness put Brar in a dilemma. He was torn between his strong desire to opt out of the rat race to do something on his own, and the wish of his dying friend, who was also his mentor, adviser, elder brother all rolled into one. When businessmen were known to axe executives in favour of the family, Dr Singh had done just the opposite, reposing all his faith and confidence on Brar. Till a few months before Dr Singh's death, Brar had still not decided which course to take.

In March 1999, Dr Singh and Brar had gone to Simla for a special conference for the senior managers of the company on how to drive growth. The session was being conducted by Sumantra Ghoshal, professor of strategic and international management, London Business School, a leading business thinker and a writer of repute.

Just before the conference was to begin, Ghoshal confronted Brar. He said that he could not talk on growth because there were apprehensions in the minds of people about what was going to happen to Ranbaxy after Dr

Singh. He wanted Brar to clarify his position. Without being emotional, he told Brar that there were 7,500 people and their families working for Ranbaxy that he had to take care of. The hard talk helped Brar make up his mind. He would put aside all his plans of retirement at fifty and work for the company.

At a meeting of the Ranbaxy board in April 1999, Dr Singh unveiled his succession plans. He said that a post of vice-chairman would be instituted to conduct meetings in future, because his failing health would prevent him from being present for all the board meetings. He wanted Khanna to take up the new post. Unknown to others, he had already decided, after discussing the matter with Brar, that Khanna should become the chairman of the company after his death. He also announced that Brar would henceforth look after the operations of the company. He also came up with a draft code for corporate governance at the meeting. All these were given a final shape at the annual general meeting of Ranbaxy shareholders at Mohali on 8 June 1999, less than a month before Dr Singh's death. Dr Singh conducted the AGM with his trademark energy, not letting it show for a moment that he was in pain. He was all smiles when he introduced Brar to the media as his successor later in the day.

Not once during those emotionally charged days did Dr Singh say a word about his sons being inducted on the board of Ranbaxy, though Malvinder had joined the company by then.

*

Malvinder had become familiar with the company's functioning early in life. Whenever he was home from school on vacations, he would travel with Ranbaxy's medical representatives, riding pillion on their scooters, observing how they sold medicines to doctors and chemists. He would sit for long hours with the people who wrote the literature for new medicines. He would attend Ranbaxy functions and interact with people from various departments, trying to understand their job. At home, Dr Singh would allow him to go through various reports so that the young boy could understand the latest trends in the industry.

Malvinder was interested in finance and economics from a very early stage. When he was in college, Dr Singh encouraged him to have a mock portfolio of shares, with daily buys and sells that he would monitor every morning. On Malvinder's twenty-first birthday, Dr Singh gave him Rs 1,00,000 to actually invest in a portfolio of stocks. Malvinder bought shares in all the companies hitting the headlines those days.

Dr Singh did not force Malvinder to join Ranbaxy once he passed out of college in 1995. Instead, he encouraged

Dr Singh and Malvinder. This portrait was taken when Dr Singh was undergoing treatment for cancer of the oesophagus.

him to explore the world outside. Malvinder was keen on joining a bank and signed up with American Express (Amex) in September 1995 because of its very strong management training programme. He was given a monthly salary of Rs 3,750 with lunch coupons worth Rs 1,000. Amex then sent him to Mumbai. Instead of staying in the bungalow of his grandmother's family at Cuffe Parade, Malvinder stayed as a paying guest in Marine Drive, doing his own laundry. But Dr Singh was under pressure from his mother, and, after a few months Malvinder moved to the Cuffe Parade bungalow.

In 1995, Dr Singh acquired Mumbai-based Empire Finance, which he merged into Fortis Healthcare (derived from the Greek word for strength, forte), a company he had set up in 1993 for financing of hospitals and health insurance (he had initiated talks with the health insurance firm, Cigna, for a possible joint venture). Malvinder joined Fortis in 1995. The next year, he got admission into Duke University in the United States. Before he joined the university, Dr Singh took him and Shivinder on a cruise to the Bahamas.

In July 1997, Malvinder had come to Delhi on his way to Singapore to do his internship with Merrill Lynch. He was amongst the first in the business school to land a mid-term job and that too with a leading investment bank. He was excited and was looking forward to the assignment. That was the time Dr Singh was detected with cancer and had to leave for treatment in the United States. Malvinder left for Singapore with a heavy heart, though Shivinder was with his father right through the treatment.

Malvinder was back in the United States on 17 August, the day the first surgery was performed on Dr Singh. He then went to see his father and decided then and there to join Ranbaxy after finishing business school. Dr Singh was lying on a bed with a ventilator on his face when Malvinder announced his intent. He held Malvinder's hand and smiled. In the third week of May 1998, Malvinder joined Ranbaxy's finance department under Kaul. Shivinder later got involved with the other family business of hospitals and diagnostics.

Right through his days at business school, Malvinder was very keen to get married. He wanted an arranged marriage. Though it was widely felt that Dr Singh forced his sons to marry before his death, it was actually the other way round. Malvinder had met Japna at Brar's house and he told Dr Singh that he wanted to marry her. Though he had met her only once and that too very briefly, Dr Singh agreed. It was decided that the *roka* ceremony would be held at Beas on 25 December. The same day, Shivinder announced to his parents that he too wanted to tie the knot with Aditi, who had studied with him at St. Stephen's college. He had also secured admission into Duke University and wanted to get married before he left for the United States. Both the marriages took place in July 1998.

Soon, Japna was pregnant and Dr Singh was on cloud nine. Wherever he went for his treatment, he would pick up clothes for the baby. But he died a few months before his first grandchild was born.

*

Dr Singh remained active in business till the very end. Till he died, any mention of a problem that needed his intervention brought back the old sparkle in his eyes. The thought that his life was coming to an end did not keep him from thinking about business possibilities. Dr Singh drew up his last great plan with Raghunath Anant Mashelkar, the director-general of the Council for Scientific and Industrial Research (CSIR). There couldn't have been a sharper contrast in the backgrounds of the two friends. While Dr Singh was born into one of the wealthiest Sikh families of the country, Mashelkar had spent his formative years in abject poverty.

Mashelkar was born in the tiny village of Mashel in south Goa on 1 January 1934. When he was a year old, he was afflicted by smallpox but survived. His family moved to Mumbai in search of livelihood but his father died soon after, leaving the family without a breadwinner. Mashelkar was only six.

But his mother, Anjanitai, was a courageous woman and did menial jobs to keep the home fire burning and see her son through school. Mashelkar wore his first pair of shoes when he was twelve years old and studied under the streetlights. But he was a brilliant student and completed his graduation in chemical technology with financial help from the Sir Dorab Tata Trust. Though he wanted to take up a job, his mother encouraged him to study further. After getting a Ph.D in chemical engineering, Mashelkar joined the University of Salford in the United Kingdom where he earned a reputation for himself in the field of polymer engineering.

In 1975, Mashelkar returned to India to work in the National Chemical Laboratory of CSIR at Pune. Over the years, his efforts as a scientist were appreciated the world over and a string of awards came his way. In 1995, Mashelkar became the director-general of CSIR. Till then, CSIR had been functioning with little interaction with industry. But Mashelkar had seen the wonderful results achieved in the West through the collaboration between industry and scientific laboratories. Soon after taking over, he made it clear that CSIR would no longer function in isolation but would work in tandem with industry.

Since then CSIR has come to the rescue of Indian business quite frequently. In 1997, the Madras High Court ordered the closure of nearly 400 tanneries in Tamil Nadu on grounds of environmental pollution. A green technology developed by CSIR at a cost of Rs 2 crore helped these tanneries commence operations again a few years later. Thanks to a menthol mint developed by a CSIR laboratory, India was not only able to displace China as the world leader in the market but was also able to corner a 70 per cent share of the mint market.

Dr Singh and Mashelkar got on very well from the first day they met. Both were passionate about science and believed in the capabilities of Indian scientists. They started talking of jointly setting up a toxicity research centre, which would help Indian pharmaceutical companies conduct toxicity analysis on their drugs and bring down their development costs. Mashelkar had even identified a piece of land at Lucknow to locate the unit. However, Dr Singh died and the proposal never materialized. 'The passion with which he planned the centre never showed that his days were numbered,' Mashelkar would remember.

10

In Top Gear

By the late 1990s and the first couple of years of the new millennium, four distinct business models had emerged for Indian pharmaceutical companies, given the new patent regime which is to come into effect from 1 January 2005.

The first—and the safest option—was to stick to manufacture of off-patent medicines, sell these in India as well as export some quantities abroad. This was the model opted for by Cipla. The company had decided that its fortunes lay in India. Thus, the domestic market became its primary focus.

The next model was slightly more global in perspective. It envisaged making India a source of generic medicine for the entire world. Companies like Matrix Laboratories and Chennai-based Divi's Labs decided to take this route. This was a low-cost business model with steady returns.

A third and unique model was put in place by Nicholas Piramal. Ajay Piramal, the Indian pharmaceutical industry's takeover tycoon, realized that there was no point in fighting Big Pharma and it would make more sense to partner with these companies. He thus started positioning Nicholas Piramal as a contract manufacturer of patented medicine for companies from all over the world. The first of such deals happened in late 2003, when Piramal tied up with United States-based Advanced Medical Optics Inc. (AMO), a global leader in ophthalmic surgical devices and eye care products, to supply select components for AMO's products.

The fourth business model was perhaps the most daring. While playing on the generics opportunity, some companies decided that it wasn't enough to do copycat drugs. To be counted in the big league, it was essential that they have their own molecules. This was the growth path chosen by Dr Reddy's Laboratories and Ranbaxy.

*

Dr Nitya Nand, who joined the Ranbaxy board in 1984, was born in Lyallpur, now in Pakistan. After graduating from Government College, Lahore, and completing his post-graduation from St. Stephen's College in Delhi, he enrolled for a Ph.D programme in the department of chemical technology at the University of Bombay. After getting a doctorate degree in 1948, he went to Cambridge for another doctorate under Alexander Todd. By end-1950, with a second doctorate under his belt, he returned to India to work at the newly-established CDRI, where he worked for thirty-five years before he retired in 1985.

CDRI had been set up under the CSIR to give a boost to drug research in India. However, at the time it was set up, there was no public sector presence in the pharmaceutical sector (Hindustan Antibiotics Ltd and IDPL were set up much later). As a result, CDRI worked closely with several Indian companies, including Cipla and Unichem, from the beginning. Though Ranbaxy had established some contact with CDRI by 1963-64, it was only after Dr Singh returned from the United States in December 1968 that the two started interacting seriously.

By the early-1970s, it was evident to Dr Nitya Nand that Dr Singh was very keen to develop a strong research base for his company and that his top priority was to develop non-infringing processes for patented drugs. His seriousness, high ethical standards and soundness of knowledge left a deep impression on Dr Nitya Nand. Dr Singh would often wait till late at night for Dr Nitya Nand to finish his work and talk to him. When Dr Nitya Nand retired on 1 January 1985, both Bhai Mohan Singh and Dr Singh had attended a function organized by CDRI to honour him. During one of his visits to Delhi after retirement, Dr Nitya Nand was asked by Dr Singh to become a scientific adviser to Ranbaxy and join the company's board of directors. Dr Nitya Nand agreed. He also continued his work at CDRI under a scheme for retired scientists run by CSIR. The programme he was working on aimed at developing new molecular prototypes which could be submitted for a broad biological screening to provide new leads for drug discovery.

Dr Nitya Nand had always admired the American system where academia and the corporate world collaborated closely in research and wanted to initiate something similar in India. Otherwise scientists ended up working in a vaccum. Collaboration with the industry also fetched them the right financial rewards. He was aware that though the Ranbaxy team for new drug discovery research was trying its best to come out with a new chemical entity, it needed much greater intellectual inputs. In 1995, he went with a proposal to Mashelkar, who had become director general of CSIR, that his project should be transferred to the Ranbaxy laboratory. Mashelkar agreed. Dr Singh was delighted and work began on the molecule at Ranbaxy's laboratory in Gurgaon.

Though the programme initially sought to develop a molecule for cardiovascular disorders, studies showed that the molecule (RBx 2258) was effective for benign prostatic hyperplasia (BPH), the non-cancerous enlargement of the prostate gland. The scientists took the lead and started clinical trials for BPH. Soon, Ranbaxy had its own molecule. To honour Dr Singh's vision and drive, the molecule was called Parvosin. A few years later, Ranbaxy discovered that the name had already been registered in an east European country. The name was, therefore, changed to Pamirosin—Pami was Dr Singh's nickname.

As the cost of developing a drug through extensive clinical trials is very high—up to $600 million—it was decided that Ranbaxy should license the drug to an overseas pharmaceutical company for development. After talking to almost a dozen companies including Pfizer, Merck and Abbot, Ranbaxy finally zeroed in on Schwarz Pharma AG, a company headquartered at Monheim, Germany.

The company was founded in 1946 by Dr Anton Schwarz, a pharmacist. It began to strengthen its competence in nitrates, medicines used to treat heart disease, in the 1950s. After the first launch of a nitrate product called Isoket 5 in 1963, Schwarz Pharma's reputation as a nitrate specialist grew further in the 1980s with the launch of more products like the mono-nitrate Elantan in 1981 and the nitroglycerin patch Deponit in 1983. During the 1980s, Schwarz also strengthened its position as a specialist for cardiovascular drugs with the launch of Cardibeltin in 1980, Tensobon in 1983 and finally a prostaglandin by the name of Prostavasin in 1985. In the 1990s, Schwarz grew rapidly with several successful acquisitions in Europe as well as the United States. By 2002, it had achieved global sales of 964 million euros, 75 per cent of which came from markets outside Germany.

By the time talks were initiated with Schwarz, Malvinder had come to head the out-licensing department of Ranbaxy. He had to drive the deal to its logical conclusion, though Brar, Kaul and Jag Mohan Khanna helped him at every step. His first meeting with the Schwarz representatives took place in May 2001 in Germany. On 19 December that year, the two parties agreed on the broad parameters of the deal including things like royalties and milestone payments. The next day, a second daughter was born to Malvinder. Everything seemed to be going fine for him.

He had given a commitment to the company's investors that the deal would be wrapped up by June 2002. After the December agreement, the Schwarz brass including CEO Patrick Schwarz came to India to check out the Ranbaxy facilities and carry the negotiations forward. In May, Malvinder, Brar and Tempest travelled to Germany for the final negotiations. On 29 June, the deal was finally signed. When Ranbaxy faxed the agreement to Germany from Brar's office, it was a poignant moment for both Brar and Malvinder. Both of them hugged each other. They had fulfilled Dr Singh's dream.

Under the terms of the deal, Schwarz Pharma agreed to pay Ranbaxy a total of $42 million over the next five to six years. This included an upfront payment of $6.3 million given successful development of the molecule, followed by royalties on commercialization. The agreement also provided for Ranbaxy to manufacture and supply finished formulations of the product to Schwarz Pharma. When the deal was struck, the compound RBx 2258 was in clinical phase II trials in India. Schwarz Pharma took over new clinical development in the United States, Europe and Japan, including further clinical phase I studies. Schwarz Pharma obtained exclusive rights to develop, market and distribute the product in the United States, Japan and Europe, while Ranbaxy retained the rights to all other markets. Schwarz Pharma gave the molecule a new code, SPM969, though it agreed to Ranbaxy's request to call it Pamirosin.

Schwarz was also excited about the acquisition. 'The compound is an uro-selective alpha-blocker which has patent protection until 2018. It belongs to the latest generation of alpha-blockers for the treatment of BPH. The aim is to develop a once-a-day formulation with rapid relief of symptoms, especially an improved efficacy on LUTS (Lower Urinary Tract Symptoms; e.g. decrease in micturition frequency at night), a low incidence of side effects and good compliance and patient acceptance,' it said in a statement after the deal was signed. 'With the new compound we are strengthening our urology pipeline,' added Prof. Iris Löw-Friedrich, member of the executive board of Schwarz Pharma.

One reason for the excitement was the growing market for anti-BPH drugs. The worldwide BPH market in 2001 amounted to $2.2 billion. In the United States, Europe and Japan—the territories with Schwarz Pharma—more than 51 million men in the forty-plus age group suffered from BPH and the BPH market for SPM969 had a volume of $2 billion with double-digit growth rates. Due to ageing, the patient population was estimated to grow by 1.5 per cent a year. Ranbaxy was also aware that the drug had huge possibilities. Tamsolocin, a similar product developed by Yamamuchi of Japan and marketed in the United States by Abbot, was logging annual sales of $600 million. Ranbaxy was confident that its Pamirosin was as good as this drug.

Ranbaxy next signed a deal with another German company, Bayer, for a new drug delivery system developed by it.

*

Bayer was started in 1863 as a maker of synthetic dyestuff. Between 1881 and 1913, Bayer developed into a chemical company with international operations. Although dyestuffs remained the company's largest division, the company was venturing into new fields and the company also set new standards in industrial research. Bayer's research efforts gave rise to numerous intermediates, dyes and pharmaceuticals, including the 'drug of the century', Aspirin, which was developed by Felix Hoffmann and launched in 1899.

Bayer's rapid growth came to a grinding halt during the First World War, when the company was cut-off from its major export markets, and sales of dyes and pharmaceuticals dropped. The company also lost most of its foreign assets. However, Bayer made it relatively smoothly through the uneasy post-war period until the stabilization of Germany in 1923-24.

Once the global economy stabilized in the mid-1920s, it became clear that the German dyestuffs industry would be unable to regain its old position in the world market. In order to remain competitive and gain access to new markets, several such companies decided to merge in 1925. Bayer transferred its assets to I.G. Farbenindustrie AG (I.G.) and was deleted from the commercial register as a company. After Germany's defeat in the Second World War, the Allied Forces confiscated I.G. in November 1945 and placed all its sites under the control of Allied officers. The company was to be dissolved and its assets made available for war reparations. However, it was finally decided to break I.G. into twelve new companies. One of these was Farbenfabriken Bayer AG, which was established on 19 December 1951.

The reconstruction of Bayer was closely linked with the 'economic miracle' in the then Federal Republic of Germany (West Germany). The Second World War had again resulted in Bayer losing its foreign assets, including its valuable patents. Rebuilding Bayer's foreign business was, clearly, important. In 1946, while still under Allied control, Bayer began to re-establish its sales activities abroad. By the 1950s, the company was allowed to acquire foreign affiliates as well. Bayer acquired the North American self-medication business of Sterling Winthrop in 1994. This was a milestone in the company's history, as the purchase also allowed the company to regain the rights to the 'Bayer' company name in the United States and use the Bayer Cross as its corporate logo. Over the years, Bayer came out with several products, including the cardiovascular drug Adalat in 1975 and ciprofloxacin in 1981.

Once the Ranbaxy research and development team had successfully come out with Pamirosin, Dr Singh made another demand: he now wanted Khanna and his team to come up with some products in the field of new drug delivery systems. Unlike the discovery of a new chemical entity, this involves altering the intake of a drug for better efficacy. The research and development team too was craving for a new blockbuster after cefaclor.

The company targeted ciprofloxacin, which had global sales of $1.4 billion in 1999. The drug was administered twice a day. Patients frequently forgot to take the second dose, which reduced the impact of the drug. Khanna led his team in developing a dosage form that required the drug to be taken only once a day. This would give a new lease of life to ciprofloxacin. A once-a-day product would lead to better compliance and, hence, better results. Around the same time, on Khanna's recommendation, Ranbaxy had appointed Prof. John Stamifortch of the University of Bath, whose area of expertise was drug delivery, as an adviser. He advised the research and development team on their new project. Soon, Ranbaxy had managed to develop a new dosage form for ciprofloxacin. Bayer, which was the innovator of ciprofloxacin, had been trying to develop a once-a-day dosage form of the drug. But Ranbaxy was able to breast the tape before it.

Once Ranbaxy had its once-a-day ciprofloxacin ready, it knew that there would be only one buyer for it, Bayer. Chattaraj had come to Delhi for a brainstorming session in September 1997. The company felt that the new product should be sold to the American arm of Bayer as the United States market was the ultimate barometer of success. Chattaraj was asked to make the first phone call to David Ebbsworth, who was heading Bayer US.

Bayer was instantly interested. It made sense for it to terminate its own research effort and buy the technology from Ranbaxy. Apart from cutting down its development costs, this would also reduce the time to take the new product to the market.

Soon, Chattaraj, Khanna and Sood were on their way to the Bayer office at Park Lane in New York. Amongst others, they were met by Bayer's worldwide marketing head for ciprofloxacin and the company' patent attorney. As talks progressed, the Bayer executives realized that the Ranbaxy team had indeed come with the very product that their own research and development team had been trying to develop. Yet, under pressure from their own scientists who hardly appreciated being beaten by an Indian company, they wanted to see the product for themselves. Thus, Khanna had to conduct a full demonstration inside the Bayer laboratory at Connecticut. With the demonstration working out to Bayer's satisfaction, the Ranbaxy team was hoping that a deal would be finalized right away. But Bayer was unwilling to make a commitment and asked for time to evaluate the proposal.

Khanna, however, was unwilling to come back without a word of confirmation from Bayer. He told the Bayer brass that he did not have much time as he had to take the same offer to other pharmaceutical companies in the United States. If Bayer was serious about buying the product, it could give Ranbaxy $1 million and the Indian company would not talk to any other company for the next four months. After some frantic phone calls to the Bayer headquarters in Germany, Khanna was given a cheque for $500,000; he agreed to keep the whole thing under wraps for the next three months. After spending three weeks in the United States, Khanna returned to Delhi. On seeing the cheque, everybody knew that it was only a matter of time before Bayer bought it.

That is what precisely happened. Bayer offered to buy Ranbaxy's once-a-day ciprofloxacin for $55 million and raised it to $65 million plus royalties on sales, following some bargaining on Ranbaxy's part. The deal was signed in June 1999, with Bayer paying $10 million at the time. Recognizing Khanna's efforts in first developing the product and then working out the deal with Bayer, Dr Singh had insisted that the final deal papers be signed by Khanna on Ranbaxy's behalf. The product was put through clinical trials immediately by Bayer and was launched in the United States in mid-2003.

Thanks to the once-a-day ciprofloxacin connection, Ranbaxy struck another deal with Bayer in 2000 when it bought out Basics GmbH, a company in which Bayer had placed its generics business. Ranbaxy was aware that Bayer was offloading this company. Though its sales of only $4 million would not give Ranbaxy a critical mass, the company would gain an entry into the huge German market for pharmaceuticals. Because of its association with Bayer, Basics GmbH's name was well respected in the market. Besides, Ranbaxy did not have to spend a large sum on the acquisition, as it was a small outfit. Due to the excellent rapport between the two companies, Bayer let Ranbaxy run Basics from its offices for almost nine months.

The acquisition orchestrated Ranbaxy's entry into the German generic market, the third largest in the world. Its generic product portfolio covered a wide therapeutic range such as cardiovascular, anti-diabetes, metabolic disorders, anti-infective drugs, analgesics and anti-rheumatics, and gastrointestinal. By 2002, Basics GmbH consolidated its operations in Germany by achieving sales of $9.01 million.

In June 2002, Ranbaxy acquired Veratide, an anti-hypertensive brand, from Procter & Gamble Pharmaceuticals Germany GmbH. In July, Basics began marketing the brand, which augmented Basics' growing cardiovascular product portfolio. Veratide commanded good brand equity with a 37 per cent market share in the category and was extensively used for management of hypertension.

After showing its skills in coming out with new chemical entities and new drug delivery systems, it was now time for Ranbaxy to show its skills in generics.

*

The short-lived tie-up with Eli Lilly not only gave Ranbaxy an entry into the United States market but also helped Ranbaxy develop ceturoxime axetil, which gave it sales of over $100 million in the United States in 2003.

Eli Lilly and Glaxo had collaborated for the development of cephalosporins. While Eli Lilly had come out with cefaclor, Glaxo had cephalexine. But by the early-1990s, the collaboration had started falling apart. Eli Lilly had been trying to develop its ceturoxime axetil, an anti-infective used to treat infections caused by bacteria, for quite some time. But Glaxo had fortified it very well with a string of patents and Eli Lilly was unable to pierce the wall. Glaxo had a patent on the drug till June 2003.

Eli Lilly had passed on the project to Ranbaxy in 1994. It took Ranbaxy no less than five years to break through Glaxo's ring of patents. On going through the patent papers, it realized that Glaxo's patent was for substantially amorphous ceturoxime axetil. On checking with various patent attorneys, Ranbaxy found that 'substantially amorphous' could have only meant over 90 per cent amorphous. If Ranbaxy could make less amorphous, or more crystalline, ceturoxime axetil, it could break through Glaxo's patents.

Ranbaxy scientists found out that Glaxo had not included milling in the string of process patents it had on the drug. So it first tried to use this process to make crystalline ceturoxime axetil. While on a trip to the United States, Rajiv Malik, who had joined the company in 1983, procured a tabletop machine and installed it in a friend's basement, hoping it would give him crystalline ceturoxime axetil. The results were disastrous. Ranbaxy tried to obtain technology from all over the world to make crystalline ceturoxime axetil but in vain.

Ranbaxy's scientists finally noted that the Glaxo patents did not cover the process of solvent precipitation to make the drug. This route was very difficult and they had earlier rejected it. Seeing this as their last hope, they decided to give it another try. It got them the desired results.

When Ranbaxy published its results, Glaxo said that the ceturoxime axetil so produced was not the same as its drug as it was crystalline. On 30 July 2001, a team led by Malik met up with representatives from the US Pharmacopoeia to prove the bio-equivalence of Ranbaxy's ceturoxime axetil. Glaxo, on its part, raised all possible objections. After a few more meetings, the US Pharmacopoeia finally gave its verdict: Ranbaxy's crystalline ceturoxime axetil was bio-equivalent to Glaxo's ceturoxime axetil.

This was not the only resistance put up by Glaxo. In September 2000, after it had merged with SmithKline Beecham to form GSK, it had notified the USFDA about its ceturoxime axetil. In December, GSK got a preliminary injunction against the Ranbaxy drug from a district court in New Jersey. But Ranbaxy went in appeal against the order in the federal court, which upheld the appeal and referred the matter back to the district court. The USFDA gave its green signal on 15 February 2002, and Ranbaxy launched its drug in May. In a little over a year, Ranbaxy's ceturoxime axetil notched up a market share of 85–90 per cent, recording sales of over $100 million. In the process, it became Ranbaxy's first product in the United States market to record a turnover of $100 million. The sales slowed down a bit once the patent on GSK's ceturoxime axetil expired on 27 June 2003, and generic versions of the drug were launched. Incidentally, the patents registered by Ranbaxy to develop crystalline ceturoxime axetil give due credit to Eli Lilly scientists.

This wasn't the last of Ranbaxy's fights with GSK in the United States. They next locked horns over the latter's blockbuster, Augmentin. In mid-2002, GSK filed a legal suit in Broomfield against Novartis and its subsidiaries, Geneva Pharmaceuticals and Biochemie, and another one in Philadelphia against Teva and Ranbaxy, alleging that there was a high probability that a bacteria used by these companies to develop generic versions of Augmentin was stolen from its laboratories. Though the lawsuit did not say that any of these companies were involved in the theft, it mentioned that the bacteria was stolen by a former GSK employee. GSK argued that the companies used the stolen bacterial strain—which it called a trade secret—to produce potassium clavulanate, which, in combination with the antibiotic amoxycillin, made up Augmentin. Ranbaxy refuted the charge. It had purchased potassium clavulanate from DSM of The Netherlands. GSK ought to have taken up the matter with the Dutch company, it argued.

The lawsuit could have been initiated to serve another purpose. GSK's sale of Augmentin in 2001 was roughly worth $1.8 billion, making it the company's second-largest-selling item, after its Seroxat antidepressant. But the company's patent on the drug in the United States was to expire in 2002, after seventeen years. The company had extended it by another seventeen years in order to protect the huge profits it was making on the drug. However, in early-2002, the three remaining patents protecting Augmentin were invalidated by a federal district court after Geneva Pharmaceuticals, Teva and Ranbaxy had filed a petition to this effect.

Securities analysts had started predicting that the sale of less expensive generic forms of Augmentin would dramatically cut into GSK's sales and earnings for 2002. Generic versions of the drug were already on sale in Europe. The pharmaceutical industry had just seen the case of Prozac, Eli Lilly's antidepressant drug, which saw a sharp erosion in sales in the United States within weeks of its patent expiring, because of the onslaught by generics.

Geneva, Teva, Lake and Ranbaxy had all got USFDA approval to launch Augmentin. Even as hearing on GSK's lawsuit about the stolen bacteria was going on, a district court abridged one patent expiring in December 2002 to

July 2002. While Geneva, Teva and Lake went ahead and launched their Augmentin, Ranbaxy did not, as it suspected that the decision might be reversed and the resulting damages could be substantial. By the time it entered the market, it had been overtaken by the other three. Ranbaxy decided to be cautious on this occasion.

The other abbreviated new drug application (ANDA) filings by Ranbaxy sailed through smoothly. By mid-1990s, it had started targeting big drugs that were going off-patent. One such drug was simvastatin, a lipid-lowering Merck drug with annual sales of $6 billion ($4.5 billion in the United States alone). The patent on the drug was to expire in 2003 but Merck had got it extended by three years to 2006. Again, Merck had registered very good process patents for the drug, which few could break.

Yatinder Kumar, who was driving the simvastatin project at Ranbaxy, knew that the only way his team of four scientists could come out with a new process was by trying something which was not too obvious and looked silly at first; something which did not make much sense in traditional chemistry and had a very low probability of success. Success came after almost two years. Merck had patented a six-step process to make the drug. Yatinder Kumar decided to try a shorter three-step process. At a very low temperature, this new process yielded simvastatin that was comparable to that of Merck. Ranbaxy quickly filed for four patents on the new process as well as for the new intermediaries so developed.

However, Ranbaxy was not the only generics company to have spotted the opportunity. Teva too had been working on the drug and had got USFDA approval to first launch the drug once the patent on it expired, though the company had been sued by Merck for infringing on a process patented by it. On going through the Teva filings with USFDA, Ranbaxy found that it had filed for 5 mg, 10 mg, 20 mg and 40 mg strengths. It had not filed for 80 mg strength. Seeing the window of opportunity, Ranbaxy quickly filed for simvastatin 80 mg. Luck turned in its favour. Soon, the simvastatin market in the United States started shifting in favour of the 80 mg dosage and this accounted for almost 60 per cent of the market by the end of 2002.

There was also no legal action against Ranbaxy after it got USFDA approval to launch ganciclovir, a Roche drug indicated for AIDS patients who have lost their immunity, with a 180-day exclusivity. Ranbaxy first sent a detailed letter to Roche explaining why its ganciclovir did not infringe upon any of the processes patented by Roche. On Roche's request, it even sent samples of the drug. The patent expired in June 2003 and Ranbaxy launched the product in end-August. Since it did not have very high sales—around $40 million in a year—it was not big enough to catch the eye of the other generics companies.

*

Bill Clinton flanked by Malav and Brar
at the Ranbaxy R&D centre at Gurgaon.

On the morning of 3 June 2003, Tom McKillop, the chief executive of Swedish pharmaceutical major AstraZeneca Plc, told journalists over breakfast at the Taj Mahal hotel in New Delhi that drug discovery costs do not vary much across countries. Thus, locating pharmaceutical research and development in India would not lead to cost savings. AstraZeneca had announced a couple of days before that it would invest $40 million in its facility in Bangalore to develop a new molecule for the treatment of tuberculosis. Now McKillop was saying the decision had little to do with the lower manpower costs in India. 'It has more to do with the availability of scientific talent in India,' he said, adding, 'The equipment and the infrastructure is the same whether the research is carried out here or abroad. The wages might be slightly lower in India but that does not make a sizeable impact.'

A few hours later, in the same hotel, Barbhaiya, then head of Ranbaxy's R&D, stunned the same set of journalists by saying that Ranbaxy could carry out new drug discovery research at one-fifth the cost of the global pharmaceutical companies. Ranbaxy was capable of developing a new chemical entity for as little as $120–180 million against the $500–900 million that it would cost in the West. This, Barbhaiya elaborated, would be achieved by employing a model built around superior risk management and cost-effectiveness. While superior risk management could help save around $130–200 million, the company could save another $160–300 million on labour arbitrage (getting the work done by cheaper Indian scientists) and $140–220 million due to operational effectiveness. The three factors together would give Ranbaxy an advantage of $430–750 million over its global competitors.

A pharmaceutical company is only as good as its head of research. During the days when Khanna was leading Ranbaxy's research and development team, it progressed gradually from evolving new process technologies to making generic products to discovery of new chemical entity and new drug delivery systems. He had been given two extensions when he reached the retirement age. Ranbaxy had started looking for his successor and Barbhaiya was one of the several scientists on the shortlist.

Barbhaiya was literally born into the world of pharmaceuticals. His physician father, Harshad C. Barbhaiya, used to work for the Sarabhais. After getting his MSc. degree from the Gujarat University at Vadodara, Barbhaiya joined the University of London in 1974 to complete his Ph.D. Four years later, in 1978, a chance meeting with Edward Garrett, a renowned professor of medicine from the University of Florida in the United States, changed Barbhaiya's life forever.

Garrett had come to London to interview Barbhaiya after he had submitted his Ph.D thesis. During lunch the same day, he asked Barbhaiya about his future plans. At that time, Barbhaiya wanted to come back to India. Garrett then chided him for not capitalizing on the work he had put in at London. 'Will you get to do this kind of work in India? You must come to the United States,' he told Barbhaiya. Barbhaiya asked him bluntly: 'Can you offer me a position?' Garrett put his hand on Barbhaiya's shoulder: 'Son, you've got a deal.' Soon after, Barbhaiya enrolled at the University of Florida.

When Ranbaxy first sounded him out, Barbhaiya was running his own consultancy, Dynametics Consulting, out of Pennington in New Jersey. He had left Bristol-Myers Squibb on 15 August 2001 after working there for twenty years. 'It was my own "*Azadi ka din* (day of independence)",' he had then joked. Starting as a senior research scientist, he had risen to become vice-president (metabolism and pharmacokinetics) by the time he left the company, managing a research budget of $30 million and 180 scientists at four sites.

Bristol-Myers Squibb had diligently built its reputation

over 140 years. It was born in 1887, when William McLaren Bristol and John Ripley Myers decided to sink $5,000 into a failing drug manufacturing firm called the Clinton Pharmaceutical Company, in Clinton, New York. The company's first nationally recognized product was a laxative mineral salt that, when dissolved in water, reproduced the taste and effects of the natural mineral waters of Bohemia. Christened Sal Hepatica, the new product sold modestly for eight years. Then, between 1903 and 1905, sales suddenly multiplied tenfold. Another runaway success of this era was Ipana toothpaste, the first toothpaste to include a disinfectant in its formula, thus providing protection against the effects of bleeding gums. The demand for Sal Hepatica and Ipana transformed Bristol-Myers from a regional company into a national company and then an international one. In 1989, Bristol-Myers had merged with Squibb, creating a global leader in the healthcare industry. The merger created what was then the world's second-largest pharmaceutical enterprise. Squibb was founded in 1856 by Edward Robinson Squibb in Brooklyn, New York, and was dedicated to the production of consistently pure medicines. This remained the company's guiding philosophy for all the years to come.

Barbhaiya left all this to start on his own. One day, he got a call from Brar asking him over for tea. The two met at the Waldorf Astoria in New York and Brar made Barbhaiya an offer to join Ranbaxy. Though he had spent his entire professional career in the United States, Barbhaiya was no stranger to Ranbaxy—he had bagged the Ranbaxy Award for Excellence in pharmaceutical research in 1993. Moreover, he had distinctly Indian tastes and passions like cricket. He would regularly go to Canada to watch India-Pakistan matches. Besides, he was a trained Hindustani classical vocalist. After several meetings with Brar in the United States as well as in India, Barbhaiya agreed to first act as a consultant to Ranbaxy. In this capacity, he made two visits to India in November 2001 and January 2002.

By then, he was struck by Ranbaxy's seriousness of intent. A few months later, he was on the company's rolls. 'I was taken in by the talent here, the hunger for success, the drive and the passion. All these people needed was someone who had done it all and could give a direction,' he said shortly after taking over as Ranbaxy's head of research and development.

Nobody could have been better aware than Barbhaiya of the dilemma facing global pharmaceutical research and development. The costs of discovering a new drug had risen steadily over the last few years and productivity was declining sharply. While Big Pharma with its large research and development budgets could afford to take a broad sweep, smaller companies like Ranbaxy had to be focussed in their efforts. They had to derive maximum profitability out of every dollar spent on research and development. In other words, Barbhaiya had to identify drugs that could be developed at low cost and in a short time.

The first decision Barbhaiya took was to narrow the focus of Ranbaxy's new drug discovery programme to five therapeutic segments: infections, metabolic disorders, urology, inflammations and respiratory diseases. This meant that the company would no longer carry out active research in drugs relating to the central nervous system, cardiovascular ailments and cancer, though it had made significant progress in anti-cancer research. The five areas on Barbhaiya's shortlist had several advantages for a company like Ranbaxy. All of them involved easy targets in the human body for the drug to attack. The clinical trials for these drugs were simple and short. In the case of anti-infective drugs, for example, results started showing up in a few weeks. Above all, there was not much competition in some of these areas. Big Pharma, for instance, had more or less given up anti-infective research and development.

Barbhaiya then decided that Ranbaxy would restrict its chase of new molecules. Instead of building a huge library of potential candidates for development, the company would work with 'precedented' targets—molecules which are already known and tested. Most of the world's blockbuster drugs have actually come out of such research. When Khanna was at the helm of affairs, he had initiated a move to acquire a laboratory in the United States to carry out early discovery work on new chemical entities. The idea was to leverage on the United States's proven skills in the early identification of new molecules and then pass it on to the Indian laboratory for later discovery work in order to benefit from the lower manpower costs. With the focus now shifting to precedented targets, Barbhaiya called off the exercise.

One way to improve the productivity of research is to reduce the risks of failure. To hedge against such risks, Ranbaxy under Barbhaiya started monitoring the early

Malav and Brian Tempest at the Ranbaxy factory at Mohali.

development potential of all its molecules. Ranbaxy had out-licensed its first new chemical entity to Schwarz. Under Barbhaiya, Ranbaxy had drawn up plans to develop a molecule fully and bring it to the market on its own by 2008.

Development of new chemical entities was only one of the three priority areas Barbhaiya identified. The other two areas were development of new drug delivery systems and the development of generic products. Generics were to be the backbone of Ranbaxy's growth. The company was already present in the world's largest generics market—the United States—and had acquired a toehold in Germany through the Basics acquisition. It was also seeking an entry into Japan.

In a very short time, Barbhaiya had changed the face of Ranbaxy's research and development. It was no longer focussed on making copycat drugs; instead, it had started resembling a Big Pharma company with its own programme to develop new chemical entities.

*

In 2002, Ranbaxy proved that it was once again thinking ahead of competition when, in September of that year, it picked up a 10 per cent stake in Nihon Pharmaceutical Industry Co. from its parent, the Tokyo-based Nippon Chemiphar Co. The business alliance was meant to get Ranbaxy and the two Japanese companies working together to launch Ranbaxy's ethical and drug delivery system-based products and generic products in Japan. In return, they would help Ranbaxy manufacture and launch Nippon Chemiphar's products in overseas markets.

A medium-size pharmaceutical company in Japan (recording sales of $168 million in the year ending March 2003, with assets of over $200 million), Nippon Chemiphar was established in 1950. As an independent pharmaceutical company, it had nearly 250 medical representatives and about sixty researchers on its rolls, engaged in research and development of new pharmaceutical products. Its products covered the therapeutic areas of central nervous system, digestive disorders, cardiovascular ailments and ulcer. Nippon Chemiphar had tweaked its business strategy in the last few years to penetrate not only the discovery of new drugs but also the generic drug market in Japan. It knew that it would be able to grow its generics business rapidly as the Japanese government would take steps to contain the soaring healthcare costs of its rapidly ageing population.

The acquisition of a stake in Nihon was yet another calculated move on Ranbaxy's part. Over the years, Japan had not only emerged as Asia's most mature pharmaceutical market, it had also become the world's second largest market with annual drug sales of $57 billion. But the cost of medicine was extremely high as generic versions of patented drugs were almost non-existent; generics accounted for only 5 per cent of the market. Unlike other pharmaceutical markets in the world, Japanese doctors also dispense medicines directly to patients. Thus, they have a vested interest in prescribing expensive patented medicine.

However, like in the United States and Europe, in Japan too, a strong movement was building up to bring down the cost of medicines. Though very little had moved by the time Ranbaxy tied up with Nihon, it was clear that it was just a matter of time before the Japanese government would also take steps to promote the production of generic medicine.

The alliance with Nihon gave Ranbaxy an unbeatable first mover's advantage. At that time, there was only one other company, E. Merck, which had set up business operations for generic medicine there. The shareholders' agreement provided for Ranbaxy increasing its stake up to 50 per cent after three years, if it wanted to. Clearly, Ranbaxy had adopted a wait and watch approach. If the generics market showed signs of explosive growth at the end of three years, it could hike its stake and take full control.

*

Malvinder was only twenty-six years old when Dr Singh passed away. All of a sudden, immense responsibilities were placed on his young shoulders. Not only did he have to take care of the family's interests in Ranbaxy, he also had to look after the fledgling healthcare business his father had set up. Besides, there was his career at Ranbaxy to worry about. His first couple of years in the company were spent in launching the 'Blue R' range of generic products for the rural and upcountry markets, the Rextar force to rejuvenate products more than ten years old and the website Ranbaxyfordoctors.com. Then he was appointed director, global licensing and business development. It was here that he first made a mark when he wrapped up the Schwarz deal. Soon after, he was asked to handle his first crisis.

Around Christmas in 2000, Peter Burema, who had replaced Tempest as regional director for Europe, noticed certain financial irregularities in Ranbaxy's London office. On investigating further, he found that some key functionaries had siphoned off company funds by underinvoicing sales and transferring the money to their own accounts.

Malvinder was dispatched to London at two days' notice to handle the crisis. He immediately moved the courts and got their accounts frozen. Criminal investigations were also launched against them. Fearing imprisonment, all the accused agreed to come clean. Ranbaxy recovered most of the money and struck off all those involved from the company's rolls.

Malvinder stayed there for three months. Working round the clock, he talked to Ranbaxy's channel partners in the country and was able to bring things under control. This established his managerial skills. Ranbaxy responded to the crisis by strengthening its internal audit system and also implemented a SAP-based enterprise resources management programme, which would help it monitor any irregularity. Even the human resources development department strengthened its assessment tools, especially for ethical conduct.

Ranbaxy was to run into problems in UK again in 2003 and 2004. In December 2003, the National Health Service (NHS) had initiated legal proceedings against seven companies, including Ranbaxy UK Ltd, for overcharging for the supply of penicillin. In its paper submitted to the high court, NHS had said that these companies had curtailed the supply of the drug to it.

In June 2003, the NHS sought compensation of at least £100 million from two companies—Ranbaxy UK Ltd and Generics UK Ltd, a subsidiary of Merck of Germany—for overcharging on the supply of rantidine, an anti-ulcer drug, from 1997 to 2000. This was the biggest claim ever made by NHS and significantly higher than the cumulative sales of £35 million reported by Ranbaxy in UK between 1997 and 2000.

Towards the end of 2001, Malvinder wanted to try out something more challenging. By now, India had become the most complex pharmaceutical market in the world. Indian scientists had developed remarkable strengths in process technologies. All blockbuster drugs of the world started being produced in India, thanks to the favourable patent regime. Hyderabad had emerged as the country's bulk drugs capital. As IDPL, the pioneer in bulk drugs in the country, was based there, several of its scientists later started out on their own in the city—the biggest success story being Dr K. Anji Reddy of Dr Reddy's Laboratories.

*

Armed with a bachelor's degree in science from Andhra Christian College, Guntur, Dr Reddy completed his BSc.

(Tech.) in pharmaceutical science from the University of Mumbai and Ph.D from the National Chemical Laboratory, Pune. Dr Reddy had six years experience in IDPL in the manufacture and implementation of new technologies in bulk drugs before he left in 1973. After leaving IDPL, he pioneered a number of bulk drugs, before he went on to form Dr Reddy's Laboratories in 1984. Over the years, the company earned a name for itself in the world generics market, especially in the United States, even as it kicked off its programme for the development of a new molecule. It became the first Indian company to out-license a molecule when it struck a deal with Norway-based Novo Nordisk, the world leader in diabetes treatment. It subsequently out-licensed two more molecules—one to Novartis and the other to Novo Nordisk.

Though the multinational pharmaceutical companies initially saw the Indian bulk drug companies as a nuisance, they soon realized their worth. It had been noticed for several years that as soon as the patent on a drug expired, its price would fall sharply as other companies would launch the same drug. At times, the fall would be as steep as 80 per cent. This made companies look at the cheapest source for these drugs. This is where Indian bulk drug producers fitted in perfectly. By the end of the 1990s, several overseas pharmaceutical companies had India on their radar screen.

Thus, when United States-based Scherring Plough's patent on loratadine expired in 2002, it started negotiating with Delhi-based Morepen Laboratories, for buying the drug from it. By then, Morepen had already got into an agreement with Geneva Pharmaceuticals, which had the right to first launch loratadine after the expiry of the patent. Once Geneva's exclusivity ended, Ranbaxy and Genpharm also got permission to launch loratadine in the United States. Genpharm also wanted to source the drug from Morepen, while Ranbaxy would be producing its own. In other words, the entire generic loratadine supply for the United States was to come from India.

The change in the Patent Act in 1970 to allow process patents had resulted in thousands of pharmaceutical companies emerging in India. Though India accounts for only 1.2 per cent of the world drugs market, it has over 20,000 registered pharmaceutical companies. The market leader in 2002, GSK, had a less than 6 per cent share of the market. Within a couple of months of the launch of a new product, there would be at least five other brands available in the market. In less than a year, there would be more than fifty competing brands. By 2000, most Indian companies had come to realize that the window of opportunity to launch clones of patented drugs would shut on 1 January 2005. This set off frenetic activity in the industry and 2002 saw over 1,000 brands launched in the country. The count was equally high in 2003. In other words, drug companies had very little lead-time for brand building. This made India the most fiercely competitive pharmaceutical market in the world.

Between 1997 and 2002, Ranbaxy had been losing market share in India. From occupying the top slot in the early-1990s, it had fallen to the third place by 2002. Malvinder saw this as a challenge. He spoke to Brar and on 1 January 2003, Malvinder was put in charge of the India region. Infusing new blood into his team, he was able to arrest Ranbaxy's falling share of the Indian drugs market within six months and regain some of market it had lost to its competitors. Apart from fighting a fierce turf battle in the Indian market, Malvinder, working with his brother Shivinder, was also giving shape to the family's healthcare business, under Fortis Healthcare.

*

Dr Singh had placed some equity of Fortis with the Infrastructure Leasing & Financial Services (IL&FS), while

Ranbaxy held a 16 per cent stake in the venture. Once Dr Singh died, Malvinder bought both out.

First off the block in the healthcare business was the Fortis Heart Institute at Mohali. The 200-bed institute, spread over 4,00,000 sq. ft, was put up at a cost of over Rs 155 crore. The institute was conceived and designed to provide top quality cardiac care facilities for Indian patients and was benchmarked against the best international medical systems. Fortis Healthcare then announced that it would invest up to Rs 1,000 crore over the next five years to set up a chain of super-specialty hospitals in key treatment areas. Shivinder, after completing his studies in the United States, got fully involved in this business.

In the meantime, Malvinder had also acquired Ranbaxy's diagnostics business. In 1995, Ranbaxy had signed a fifty-fifty joint venture agreement with the California-based Specialty Laboratories Inc., to set up a string of clinical reference laboratories in India. This company came to be known as Specialty Ranbaxy Pvt. Ltd and was being run by Specialty, with Ranbaxy providing local assistance. However, Ranbaxy found out that Specialty was operating with very high costs, which resulted in losses right from the beginning; it reported a loss of Rs 12 crore at the end of the first year.

Alarmed, Ranbaxy offered to run the company with only technical inputs from Specialty, which the latter refused to do. As Ranbaxy saw little hope of improvement in the company's prospects, it asked Specialty to buy it out of the joint venture. Specialty responded that it was willing to pay not more than one dollar for Ranbaxy's 50 per cent stake. Miffed, Ranbaxy now said that it would buy out Specialty. After a brief arbitration in Singapore, Ranbaxy picked up Specialty's stake for one dollar. It now owned 100 per cent of the company but did not intend to stay in the field of diagnostics. Consequently, it started looking for a buyer for the company.

By now, Malvinder and Shivinder had set their healthcare

plans rolling. Their hospital at Mohali was up and running and more investments were on the drawing board. Malvinder approached Ranbaxy to buy out Specialty Ranbaxy Ltd, as he felt that diagnostics went well with the family's healthcare business. Ranbaxy could find little reason to object. Malvinder bought the company, picking up the shares from Ranbaxy at face value.

Several of Dr Singh's close friends would say Malvinder was like his father—focussed and a tough taskmaster, though humble to the core. Belonging to one of the wealthiest families in the country never showed on him. When he joined college, Malvinder used to commute by bus, though he had got his driving licence when he turned eighteen. It was only towards the end of Malvinder's first year in college, that Dr Singh bought him a motorcycle. After a year, he joined a car pool. Towards the end of his graduation, Malvinder finally got a Maruti Suzuki Gypsy, which he continued to use for many years. While many of his friends frequented the city's five-star hotels in the evenings, Malvinder would invariably head for the middle-class eating places to pick up a dosa or some other snack. Dr Singh never spoilt his children by giving them too much money to spend. While children of other businessmen got up to Rs 30,000 per month as pocket money, Malvinder got Rs 250 every month during the first and second years in college and Rs 500 in the third year.

When he joined Ranbaxy, he was aware that his colleagues felt uncomfortable working with him as he was the owner's son. It became worse after Dr Singh died; he was now the owner of the company along with his brother. To put his colleagues at ease, Malvinder ate at the Ranbaxy mess for a long time, instead of the executive dining hall where the Ranbaxy top brass took its meals.

Though not initiated into the faith, Malvinder also got deeply attached to the Radhasoami Satsang, visiting Beas eight to nine times every year. Yet, the responsibilities made him grow fast. 'At times I feel that I am living a life much older than my age. Most of the people I deal with are at least forty to forty-five years old. But then I am responsible for the family's interests. The buck stops with me,' he said soon after taking over as the head of the India region.

Within a year of taking on this position, Malvinder got his big break: the post of president (pharmaceuticals) and a position on the company's board of directors. When the announcement was made on 22 December 2003, most people saw it as the family trying to regain control of the company from Brar.

The argument was not without merit. Tempest was fifty-six years old when he was designated CEO of the company. As the retirement age at Ranbaxy is fifty-eight years, it meant that he would have a stint of only two years, after which he would have to make way for the next in command, Malvinder. By now, people had also started suggesting that though Dr Singh had not put his sons on the board, the family's interests were always well taken care of on the board through relatives and close friends. Harpal Singh, for instance, was Malvinder's father-in-law. Tejinder Khanna was a Radhasoami Satsang follower and could be counted on for his loyalty to the family. Surendra Daulat Singh and Vivek Bharat Ram were very close friends of Dr Singh.

Malvinder, on his part, maintained that his elevation to the board had nothing to do with his stake in Ranbaxy. The board membership, he said, came with the job of president.

*

Till 1999 and early 2000, when the returns on Ranbaxy's overseas investments were yet to come, many people—including many within the company—started saying that the projections made in 1994 were unlikely to materialize and that Dr Singh and Brar had got their figures wrong.

Though Brar was convinced that the projections would be met, he could hardly announce fresh targets for his team.

Fortunately for him, by 2001, he could feel that Ranbaxy would be able to achieve its target of $1 billion turnover by 2004. Starting from 1999, the company had seen signs of real innovation. By end-2003, he started talking of overshooting the target by at least 20 per cent. It was evident to other members of his core team also. They had started clamouring for the next challenge. He also had to ensure that complacency did not set in. The team had to be galvanized for the next goal.

Brar now started looking out for the next level of aspirations. He held a series of meetings with his key team to find out where they wanted to take the company after 2004. Slowly, it dawned on him that he would require the advice of professionals with an international exposure to fix the new targets. He discussed the issues with management gurus like Nitin Nohria, C.K. Prahlad, Athreya and Ghoshal and had informal consultations with top consultancy firms like Mckinsey and the Boston Consulting Group. He also spoke to healthcare experts from investment banks like Merrill Lynch and Credit Suisse First Boston. Hemant Shah too pitched in with his advice. As the United States was central to Ranbaxy's future growth plans, his views were invaluable.

After six months of discussions, Brar had a rough idea of where Ranbaxy could be headed. Along with Mckinsey, Brar's key aides in strategic thinking—Tempest and Rahul Goswami—drew up half a dozen case studies of global pharmaceutical companies that had graduated from generics to specialty products. It was now time to roll out the vision to the top functionaries of the company.

In September 2002, forty-odd Ranbaxy executives descended on Ananda Spa near Rishikesh on the banks of the Ganges. The palace was the property of the former royal family of Garhwal, which had been converted into India's first world-class spa with various 'wellness' programmes thrown in. It was in the sylvan surroundings of Ananda that Ranbaxy's grand vision was first unrolled.

It was called the Garuda Vision. The name Garuda was chosen because the distinctly Indian eagle soars over all others in the sky. It is also the national bird of the United States, where Ranbaxy was seeking its fortunes. The target for 2012 was fixed at $5 billion—a quantum jump from less than $1 billion in 2003. The company would get 40 per cent of its business from proprietory products, as against near zero in 2003. Ultimately, Ranbaxy would be among the top five generic companies in the world, as compared to its number nine position in 2003. These were stretched targets. People were told that if Ranbaxy were to achieve a turnover of $4 billion by 2012 and get 30 per cent of its turnover from proprietary products, it would still be fine.

After finalizing the vision, it was decided to wait for three months during which competency gaps were identified and plans were drawn up to plug them. Between March and July 2003, the Garuda Vision was unveiled to all 8,500 Ranbaxy employees. Brar personally addressed some 3,500 of them in New Delhi, Dewas, Bangkok and the United States.

Finally, Ranbaxy was ready for the next challenge.

Index